DISCOVERING A
DYNAMIC MARRIAGE

Him: **Dynamic Marriage** *provided the structure for us to work on our marriage more intentionally, rather than grappling around in the dark.*

Her: It was an opportunity to discuss high-conflict issues without making someone the bad guy for bringing up difficult stuff.

– D.W. & D.W.

Him: An opportunity to: 1) after forty years of marriage discuss topics we never explored in depth before, 2) focus on what works in our marriage—not what is broken, believing that expanding what works trumps what doesn't.

Her: Loved the rich opportunity to learn together with the support and encouragement of other couples.

– B.F. & K.F.

Him: Excellent! a. It gets one ready to change. b. It moved our relationship forward with communication skills we continue to use. c. It inspired us to "seek more"…other avenues to continue and reinforce what we are learning.

Her: Very valuable! Usually an avoider of relationship stuff, my husband was actually the one who initiated the homework and writing sessions! It turned our marriage around.

– S.V & J. V.

Him: We gained so much from the **Dynamic Marriage** course focused on what we already do well. It was refreshing and up-lifting to deepen our relationship celebrating past successes rather than dwelling on past failures. Understanding how our child-hood models undermined our marriage helped overcome destructive beliefs and behaviors.

Her: We feel we are still growing when we can trace a snag in our relationship to something we learned growing up in our families. Nearing fifty years of marriage and stronger than ever! God bless you…we do!

– D.C. & J.C.

Him: We learned the importance of stepping out of emotional turmoil during a conflict and metacognitively processing what is really happening between us in the moment. If either one of us has the presence of mind in the heat of battle, it helps us de-esca-late and defuse. This really works!

Her: We were able to identify unspoken expectations and mis-construed assumptions. These two things have repeatedly gotten us into conflict, but we never got down to the root cause of our struggles.

– D.W & D. W.

DISCOVERING A DYNAMIC MARRIAGE

*12 Secrets to Navigating
Uncharted Seas*

AVIVA
PUBLISHING
New York

Joy Evans Peterson, M.A.

Discovering A Dynamic Marriage: 12 Secrets to Navigating Uncharted Seas

©2012 by Joy Evans Peterson, M.A.

Address all inquiries to:
Joy Evans Peterson, M.A.
www.JoyEvansPeterson.com

ISBN: 978-1-935586-98-2

Library of Congress Control Number: 2012911244

Editor: Tyler R. Tichelaar, Ph.D.

Cover Design: Jill Neumeister, www.OrcaDesignGroup.com

Interior Layout: Fusion Creative Works, www.fusioncw.com

Printed in the United States of America

For additional copies, visit: www.JoyEvansPeterson.com

DEDICATION

Wendolyn Joy, Arnold Emanuel,
Holly Suzanne and Shannon Denise

Who inspired me with a passion
to safeguard future generations
of parents and their children
from the agony of divorce.

In Appreciation

DANA CLAUSON, BSN AND JOHN CLAUSON, D.MIN.

I am aware that the language that follows is fairly standard for tributes to helping hands in birthing a book and possibly they are always true, not merely form; I have no way of knowing. I do know that *Discovering a Dynamic Marriage* would not have been breathed to life without the devoted and skillful midwifery of Dana and John Clauson. The wisdom in this book would have languished in the womb of unwritten words…or perhaps the tomb of unexpressed thoughts. Truly!

Dana was in a group of lay counselors I trained several years ago in a local church. At my request, she and her husband John agreed to participate with two other couples in the original pilot run of Dynamic Marriage. They were astonished with the enrichment of their own solid, forty-four year marriage, and signed on to train as facilitators. They had no idea what they were taking on!

Not only did they facilitate a group of couples the following autumn with great success, but the three-hour coaching sessions preparing them for each week's class continued for the year beyond and became the groundwork for this book. Their feedback from the front-line experience of facilitating the protocol offered a hands-on edge to the book that lifted it out of the realm of theory and into the living rooms and bedrooms of couples struggling to make their marriages excellent.

Each Monday afternoon, they held me accountable. I emailed a rough draft of each chapter, and they came prepared to go over it word-by-word and line-by-line. Their feedback, input, and refinements made it a much more relevant book. Their unfailing faith and commitment kept me going when my energy was flagging and beset by demon doubt . Their stories of transformation in couples' lives inspired and kept the fire in my own belly when the embers were less than glowing.

It is my fervent prayer that over the next several decades, many thriving couples will join me in gratitude to the Clausons for their diligence and vision.

Thank you, Dana & John.

ACKNOWLEDGMENTS

Where to start...*Discovering a Dynamic Marriage* has been many years in the making, many supportive friends and two years in the writing. I would like to express my gratitude to:

- My father, who encouraged me to write for as long as I can remember...I hope he's looking down from heaven to see that I finally listened.

- My mother who modeled commitment and courage...and love...above all love.

- Ron and Dennis, who gave me beloved children and wrote huge chapters of life on my heart.

- My children, who taught me about loving someone more than life...but also more than I ever wanted to know about heartache, humility and regret.

- My adopted daughter Andrea – the busiest working mom I know - who checked in nearly every day, loved me, believed in me, and motivated me on to finish this book ... for myself, for her, and especially for my grandchildren.

- My clients, who entrusted their pain, confusion, and triumph to me for twenty-five years.

- Carol and Tim Scheck, whose marriage has inspired me for fifty years; they have always been there for me in every way that matters, time and again…and still.

- Elizabeth Bloom, my dear friend, who regularly enforced a yoga break, or rescued me for an evening away from the computer, aptly modeled by Mango, the feline master of relaxation.

- Joanna Cummings who beat me to press with ***Kick Butts & Take Names***, and inspired me to persevere.

- Lance Brown, who lured me out of retirement to develop and train lay counselors at his church…and challenged me to put pen to paper… and so much, much more.

- Dana and John, Verna and Art, Linda and Mike, who were willing guinea pigs in the trial run of Discovering a Dynamic Marriage, and felt their marriages were blessed by the experiment.

- Sammi McCubbins who believed Dynamic Marriage could help struggling couples and held me up through the grueling final stages, and took over the business end of publishing and launch.

- Patrick Snow, my writing/publishing mentor and coach…I hate to think about the missteps I would have made without his guidance, knowledge, con-

stant encouragement and stable of trusted professionals and friends in the industry.

- Howard Howell, who guides me through the maze of
  the new-fangled social media stuff I don't understand
  (and really don't want to!).

- To Dave Stave who volunteered his editing skills and
  cleaned up spelling, grammar and syntax as a labor of
  love and support. He made Tyler's job easier.

- Jill Neumeister, who caught the vision of what I
  wanted the cover art to convey and did an awesome
  job of bringing it to life.

- Tyler Tichelaar, who gleefully took on the task of editing the manuscript for content and continuity and
  offered invaluable feedback.

- To Shiloh Schroeder of Fusion who undertook the
  overwhelming task of formatting and making the
  book print-ready.

- And last but not least, Rich, my caring companion
  whose daily presence, unerring insight, sound advice
  and encouragement kept me on task and on target
  for the two year writing journey. I am a better person
  and author because of his love and support. I owe
  him much more than just my sanity.

CONTENTS

A NOTE FROM THE AUTHOR

Dear Reader,

I wrote this book not only to save you and your family from the devastation of divorce, but to help you to find the kind of satisfaction in marriage you dreamed of when you fell in love and joined your lives filled with hope and optimism. In the bloom and exuberance of youth, seldom does anyone let you in on the fact that a loving, lasting marriage doesn't automatically follow the honeymoon. Even if you witnessed an unhappy alliance between your parents, and made a series of promises to yourself about how you would avoid the behaviors and mistakes that led to their failure, there was not a navigation chart to guide you on the voyage into the unknown.

In the years you were exploring potential mating choices, the apparent options were prescribed by invisible scripts, mental models or maps, too deeply embedded to be in your awareness. And yet, in the pheromone and serotonin induced euphoria of ignorance, lifetime commitments are made, children are born, and powerful unconscious forces—whether for good or ill—dictate the course of a future you imagine you can control.

TURNING POINT MOMENT

Now you are here, seeking answers—the GPS that did not come with the marriage certificate. What will you learn in *Discovering a Dynamic Marriage* that is different from what you have read before? Get ready for a whole new paradigm, a series of seven fundamental beliefs!

1. Belief in Relationship Contracts

Every relationship has an underlying "contract," conscious or unconscious. In most cases, couples allow it to be drafted by default—like case law in the legal field; a precedent is set on a foundation of unexamined behaviors, expectations, and assumptions. A person behaves in a certain way, and unless challenged by the other, it is assumed to be acceptable. Early in a relationship, people are reluctant to confront minor irritants and issues. However, as a relationship becomes committed, these established patterns, assumptions, and expectations are already set in place, without scrutiny and mutual agreement. When resistance is finally voiced—usually under duress—the unwitting offender feels confused and humiliated.

2. Belief in Celebrating Excellence

To create a Dynamic Marriage is to make a commitment to a mutual voyage that lasts a lifetime, come what may. It is a journey toward understanding yourselves and one another, honoring the best of what already exists in your marriage, and celebrating together what is exceptional in your intentions and your actions. You will concentrate on what you do well, and identify what you want to do differently. This is not the same as approaches offering *quick fix* formulas about contrasts between genders, variations in communication styles, and altering superficial relationship behaviors and patterns. Dynamic Marriage is based on courage, self-knowledge, and perseverance. It leads to a life built on a consciously designed foundation of shared love, values, and spiritual practices.

3. Belief in the Power of Partnership!

You will start at the beginning, the *very* beginning! In the biblical account of creation, when God finished forming the Universe, He proclaimed it was good. He then charged the man, Adam, with the job of caring for all He created. Afterwards, He uttered words that still ring with truth through all the ages:

"It is not good for man to be alone."

So God created Eve to be Adam's helpmate. Traditionally, this statement has been interpreted as Adam's helper, a justification throughout history for positioning women as subservient to men. However, Scriptures repeatedly assert that God never intended or sanctioned inequality among His children; everything in Jesus' teachings supports equality for everyone. In fact, what He meant was that Eve was fashioned to be God's helper *with* Adam; his *partner* in caring for Creation.

Partnership is at the core of a satisfying marriage. A successful marriage requires a clear understanding of what constitutes a partnership—which marriage is in the eyes of the law—and mastering the skills that make marriage and all relationships successful. When you learn these skills for the sake of your marriage, you can expect these same skills to make you more effective as parents and in all interactions with people in every area of your life.

4. Belief in Equality

You will hopefully acquire a profound belief in marriage—not merely in an "institution of marriage" sense—but in honoring the strength, resilience, and tenacity of loving bonds in deeply committed relationships, as it was ordained from the very beginning.

"Love one another as God has loved us."

I also believe God's statement, "It is not good for man to be alone," has a much grander, all-encompassing message. If God were talking about the best possible caretakers for His glorious new creation, Adam *and* Eve, we must also assume the "best possible" requires both male and female perspectives in every aspect of attending to God's children, our children, and His world. The collateral benefits have far-reaching effects on all areas of life by marriage partners who are committed to equality, have experienced the benefits, and modeled it to their offspring. The richness of learning provided by mutual respect for both masculine and feminine perspectives on issues and decisions within marriage and family cannot be duplicated in any other setting or institution in our lives.

In order for the future to hold the promise of a better world—and we really cannot face life without that dream—our sons and daughters need to be equal partners, not only in marriage, but to have equal voice and opportunity in the total spectrum of life: in career, in governance, in religion, in education, in the workplace, in the law.

5. Belief in Lifelong Learning and Growth

David Schnarch,[1] in referring to marriage, uses the metaphor of a "crucible." A crucible is the vessel in which gold is refined. Gold is heated in a crucible until it melts, and the impurities—called dross—rise to the surface where it can be skimmed away, leaving purified gold behind. It is a fitting metaphor. Most often, marriage is the crucible in which the continuing growth and development of individuals takes place. Marriage is the melting pot in which hidden imperfections and impurities, childhood wounds, dysfunctional scripts, denial, and maladaptive strategies boil to the surface where they can be examined, appreciated for the purpose they served to protect or sustain us, and scrubbed away—leaving finer, wiser, humbler individuals and partners in their wake.

6. Belief in Love & Forgiveness

It is in relationships that you are confronted with not only your wounds, your losses, your flaws, and your yearnings, but also your capacity for love and forgiveness. It is in commitment that you learn to push beyond your capacity for selflessness and constancy. In bumps and bruises, disappointments and disillusionments, wrong turns, dead ends, flawed decisions, and failure, lie the seeds of wisdom and maturity.

You may never realize the boundaries of your emotional depths until you are in a relationship that is more important to you than your own life. Building a life around another and bearing children takes you to the very heart of your being. And it is in your heart that the seeds of the Divine reside, waiting for you to surrender everything to love and give it expression. The way you love and forgive the children to whom you have given life is merely a hint of the love God has for you and all He created. It is up to you to give His love expression in your relationships and in your communities.

Eben Alexander, a neurosurgeon who survived a deep week-long coma, wrote about what he saw when his brain was not functioning. His article ends with urging us "to get it right" by making love our greatest—perhaps our sole—priority:

> "This new picture of reality will take a long time to put together. In fact, reality is too vast, too complex, and too irreducibly mysterious for a full picture of it ever to be absolutely complete. But in essence, it will show the universe as evolving, multi-dimensional, and known down to its every last atom by a God who cares for us even more deeply and fiercely than any parent ever loved their child.
>
> I'm still a doctor, and still a man of science every bit as much as I was before I had my experience. But on a deep level I'm very different from the person I was before, because I've caught a glimpse of this emerging picture of reality. And you can believe me when I tell you that it will be worth every bit of the work it will take us, and those who come after us, to get it right."[1]

7. Belief in Transcendence[2]

A belief in transcendence is a belief in miracles. I once heard a miracle defined as "*a shift in perspective.*"[3] At another time, I read that all anguish is a result of being "*at war with reality*"[4] —the conviction that something should be different than it is. The Scriptures summarize all commandments in one single command: "*Love your neighbor as yourself.*"[5] The apostle Paul once said, "*I have learned to be content whatever the circumstances.*"[6] Somewhere within this minute, but profound, collection of wisdom is the answer to finding peace within and the ability to transcend any challenge or situation—even marriage—with grit and grace.

Couples don't set out to mess up their relationships and get divorced. But they don't come into marriage with a navigation chart or emotional GPS either….They are forced to muddle through as best they can. Half will end up in divorce court and carry the sense of failure the rest of their lives.

It is my hope that practicing the innovative paradigm in *Discovering A Dynamic Marriage* will wipe the slate clean and start your marriage fresh with a relationship contract—GPS—that you will author together, step-by-step.

A Final Note: The author is a Christian, and *Discovering a Dynamic Marriage* was designed to be implemented in workshops and courses offered by churches and institutions of all faiths to meet a universal need. Perhaps surprisingly, research indicates that 85 percent of couples' first point of contact when their marriage is in trouble is a clergyman or a church. The statistic encompasses the general population, including non-believers and the unchurched.

The principles in *Designing a Dynamic Marriage* are based on sacred spiritual and sound psychological principles, not on theology or doctrine. My intention is for the book to be a life-altering resource for couples whatever their spiritual beliefs. As a psychotherapist, I hold the holistic view that emotional healing cannot transpire without taking into account the spiritual dimension of an individual's life.

In my later years, I find it increasingly arrogant—for me or anyone—to assume that what I believe is the only way God works. Most of the pain and conflict in the world comes from defending this absurd assumption. I respect the various faiths and sacred traditions of my clients, friends, and colleagues. Some of my favorite profound insights and writings on marriage come from other spiritual and wisdom traditions.

I have chosen to include familiar, relevant references from the Bible, and wisdom from a diversity of other writers, sages and sacred traditions. *Discovering a Dynamic Marriage* is not a platform to promote my personal beliefs, but to serve all God's children. My mission is to save marriages and families from a lifetime of woundedness in the wake of divorce, whatever a person's belief system.

GETTING THE MOST
FROM THIS BOOK

Discovering a Dynamic Marriage is written to be used in the following ways:

1. By couples reading through it on their own.

2. As a treatment guide for a professional psychothera-pist working with a couple .

3. As the text for a course of up to twelve couples, facili-tated by a certified DDM (Discovering a Dynamic Marriage) Ambassador, usually in a church or organi-zation focused on healthy couples and families.

4. By couples going through the DDM course online webinar.

Often *Discovering a Dynamic Marriage* is launched with an all-day workshop for couples. It may be sponsored by sever-al churches or family organizations in a community. If you picked up a copy of *Discovering a Dynamic Marriage* at a workshop, you are already acquainted with how this works.

If you also acquired the *The Journey, a* companion workbook, you arc well on your way.

If you have the book and no prior introduction to the program, here are some important details to help you navigate the course. First, you need to know it requires a substantial investment of time and hard work, but it is satisfying work, not drudgery. The rewards are measured in a happy marriage and thriving family. And ultimately, it is not nearly as difficult as going through a divorce and its lifetime wake of destruction.

From the onset, become familiar with the Dynamic Marriage website: **www.DiscoveringDynamicMarriage.com**. It is a resource where you will find tips, stories from other couples, updates, calendar of events, articles, and downloads of worksheets referenced in the text.

The book is divided into twelve separate areas of marriage and clustered into broader categories covering related subjects. Part I: The Four Compass Points form the core agreements around which the entire relationship revolves. You are advised to revisit your agreements in these four areas as you negotiate the other chapters specifically devoted to a subject—especially if you find yourselves getting into conflict. Review your Compass Points to get back on course. Marriage is a voyage across uncharted seas, not a final destination.

Couples going through the course generally meet every other week for six months and reserve the same time during the off week to do the homework and write the "clause" in their agreement covering the subject at hand. If you are taking the journey on your own, you can choose to follow the six-month model or tackle one chapter per month over a year. In either case, it is important to chart your course at the onset and stick to it, including deciding on a meeting time each week that you hold sacred. Think of it as your date night.

The best plan is for each partner to have a personal copy of the book and *The Journey*. Read the chapter and highlight the passages that are particularly meaningful to you. Do the Exercises individually, as instructed, and share your answers during the discussion. Before you begin the Exercises discussion, review each chapter together and share the highlighted passages and what it is about them that speaks to you. If you elect to use *The Journey* companion workbook, you will each need to have your own. You can get them at the Dynamic Marriage Workshop or from the website.

Keep in mind that your objective throughout the process is to explore the underpinnings of your relationship beliefs and behaviors. Then to draft your personal Dynamic Marriage agreement to guide your relationship into the future.

Working separately, begin by filling out the goal sheet. What do you hope to accomplish? What does your ideal marriage look like? What are the things you most long for in your marriage? What kind of partner would you like to be? Describe in detail the partner you want to have. How do you feel about yourself, your partner, your marriage, your life? Write your answers in your book on the page provided.

Share your dreams and goals. Listen to each other with *curiosity and intention to understand.* You will be reminded of this instruction many times in the book; it is key to harmony and accord in a collaborative partnership.

Next fill out and sign the Our Commitment page.

At the end of each chapter is a blank page to list your Goals and Objectives to be covered in the contract clause for the chapter's subject. Make your lists individually on this page and discuss them before writing the relevant clause for your Dynamic Marriage Agreement.

Draft your clause on a separate paper or computer until you are agreed on the content and wording. Then each of you should copy the clause on the page provided in the book *in your own handwriting*. The way the human brain works, a deep connection occurs best when something is handwritten. The other advantage is that you each have your own handwritten clause-by-clause record of your personal relationship agreement.

Couples tend to immortalize the memories of their courtship and wedding day. But this agreement is even more significant. You are older and wiser. You have weathered many storms, rogue waves, ill winds, and rough seas. Yet here you are, still working together and committed to take yourselves and your marriage to the next level. Celebrate and keep a record of this commitment to being one of the blessed minority...an "intact family!"

OUR RELATIONSHIP GOALS

PRINCIPLES, RULES & GUIDELINES

Every relationship has an underlying "contract," conscious or unconscious. Couples allow it to be drafted by default—like case law in the legal field; a precedent is set on a foundation of unchallenged behaviors, expectations, and assumptions. A person behaves in a certain way, and if unchallenged by the other, that behavior is assumed to be acceptable. When resistance is finally voiced—under duress—the offender feels confused and humiliated.

Early in a relationship, people are reluctant to confront minor irritants or issues. However, once a commitment is made, the patterns, assumptions, and expectations are already individually set in place, without examination and mutual agreement.

Fortunately, it is never too late to craft a meaningful contract that preserves the relationship's cherished values and traditions, and replaces irritating, destructive, and ineffective feelings, behaviors, and attitudes. Engaging in a significant, life-changing dialogue about relationship priorities, reflecting and refining, and transcending the past will establish a renewed, satisfyingly new intimacy.

Rules and Guidelines for a Dynamic Marriage are a bit unusual but help ensure a successful and transformative experience:

- Growing and enriching the *relationship,* and the *people* in the relationship is the objective.

- Loving means that the beloved's needs, feelings, opinions, and happiness are as important as my own.

- Nobody wins unless everybody wins, and never at the expense of another.

- No blame or judgment of another: giving each other every benefit of the doubt.

- Treat one another with the same love and respect you want to receive.

- Listen with curiosity and *intention* to appreciate and understand.

- Seek first to understand and second to be understood.

- Honesty involves telling your truth in *this* moment, relevant to this discussion, not a hidden past.

- Ego is the defensive mask of insecurity and immaturity.

- Fear is the enemy of love and real intimacy; selfish and closed.

- When you are sure you are right or need to be—you are probably wrong (EGO is driving you).

- Every problem/issue offers myriad possibilities; the problem is limiting beliefs, feelings, attitudes.

- Miracles can be a slight shift in perspective—understanding from another's viewpoint.

Consider thoughtfully, with intentional openness to discovery. Discover what works and determine what you want to keep and create more of in your relationship. What doesn't work will fall away from lack of mutual support. Don't rehash old grievances or disagreements. Take a fresh look at what unconscious scripts and beliefs you currently operate under. Consider whether they still serve you. Rewrite, refine, and agree on how you will relate on this issue moving forward.

If an issue requires more than one session, give it the time necessary to reach agreement. Skip a loaded category and revisit it after you have space to absorb and reflect. Finding you agree on a number of issues often generates the confidence to attack really difficult ones. If you are truly stuck on an issue, seek professional help in getting to the bottom of it.

OUR COMMITMENT

We, _____, in our desire for our marriage to be all we want it to be, commit to work together for the next _____ months to make it satisfying and healthy. With humility, courage, and openness, we acknowledge that it requires us both individually and as a couple, to step out of our comfort zone to discover unhealthy patterns of relating that have been established over time. We agree to celebrate and build on those patterns that move us toward a Dynamic Marriage, to challenge and surrender feelings and behaviors that are hindrances to our goal.

- We agree to meet together for sessions _____ a month for _____ months.

- We agree to honor this special time to learn together.

- Respecting the importance of our time together we will begin and end each session on time.

- We arrive with reading and homework prepared.

- We will enter into the session relaxed and ready to share openly and honestly from the heart.

- We agree the sessions are a time for designing the future we dream of. This is NOT *bare-your-soul* or *air-dirty-linen* time or dragging up old hurts and offenses of the past.

- We confirm that neither of us has an unacknowledged or unaddressed addiction. (If you are in recovery or working a program, you may participate in the group.)

- We each confirm that neither of us is involved in a relationship with a third party—physically or emotionally.

- We mutually aspire to design a Dynamic Marriage, and are committed to Discover—the best in each other and our marriage, and Dare—the courage to do whatever is necessary to make it our intention and priority for the next _____ months.

We have read, understand, and agree to the Principles, Rules, and Guidelines, and Our Commitment:

_____ _____

Signature *Date*

_____ _____

Signature *Date*

YOUR INVITATION TO A DYNAMIC MARRIAGE

What is the title all about? Take a look at the dictionary definitions of the words in the title.

dare *(verb)[1]*

> *necessary courage or boldness for a decision, action, or behavior.*

discover *(verb)*

> *to see, learn, find, or find out; gain knowledge of, notice, realize, or create.*

dynamic *(adjective)*

> *energy or effective action; motion; ever changing and evolving.*

marriage *(noun)*

> *the agreement under which a man and woman formalize living as husband and wife by legal commitments, religious ceremonies, etc.*

A relationship in which two people have pledged to each other as husband and wife.

Putting the words together the title might be summarized as:

The courage to create

a continually evolving,

fulfilling marital relationship.

So the journey of discovery begins. As a seasoned sailor, I resonate with a seagoing metaphor for marriage. Let's imagine the courage and daring of early explorers setting out in wind-driven vessels for new lands, guided by the stars and ancient navigational charts of known seas and land masses… and vast unknowns.

When comparing the early explorers and their tools with today's pinpoint navigational information that we have from satellite images and GPS, it's almost comical. It's also a miracle that some ships in the past actually ended up where they set out to go, given the limited knowledge they had at the time.

Even with all the state-of-the-art seagoing vessels, preparation and navigation equipment, the journey is still perilous. The high seas hold many unknowns and potential dangers. Real life relationships and extended ocean voyages have much in common. The best preparation is to build the strongest relationship vessel, keep it in sea-worthy repair, expect—no, embrace—the inevitable rough seas, ride out rogue waves, and keep sailing toward a safe harbor.

The series of journeys through each of the chapters will guide you step-by-step. You will dredge up and examine—***Discover***—the old maps, and update with the relevant information you will learn. And together chart your own course—***Dare***—to the relationship you both desire—a ***Dynamic Marriage***. You are the map-makers, script-writers, and co-captains of the ship.

Welcome aboard!

Relationship Essentials

THE RIVER RUNNING THROUGH IT

These five basic needs and elements are vital to success and satisfaction in each of the twelve areas of your marriage. Spend time together discussing how each of these elements influence and reflect your relationship values and boundaries. Incorporate these elements when working through the exercises and discussion questions at the end of each chapter. Visit them again in negotiating each area of your marriage. Make sure all the essential elements are reviewed before finalizing each clause of your agreement.

SIGNIFICANCE & SECURITY

The most important need of every individual—child or adult—is to know he or she matters to someone. To the young child, it is a matter of survival. To the adult, the feeling of being essential to at least one other person gives a sense of belonging and security. It is in connection to others that people feel connected to life. In marriage, the feeling of significance to the beloved is the basis of creating a sense of security for the couple and the family.

Part of establishing a secure environment is acknowledging when something is not right in the marriage/relationship and getting it out in the open: telling your truth and behaving in a way that reflects that truth while knowing that your feelings and opinions are important to your beloved and that decisions that impact you will not be made without being a party to the process.

MEANING & PURPOSE

People's number-one fear is living a meaningless life, according to Lieder and Shapiro in *Repacking Your Bags*. The purpose of life is a life of purpose. Finding meaning and purpose in life is the most vital activity in which a person can engage. Clearly understanding what gives each spouse meaning and purpose is a standard against which to evaluate and refine all of one's activities. Purpose is power!

Meaning and purpose are exterior manifestations of the spiritual path to the center of your being and your journey. When you understand each other's purposes and journeys, you develop a profound sense of who you are as individuals and where you want to go as a couple. Supporting and appreciating each other's dreams and accomplishments brings joy in the good times and peace resting in faith during the tough times.

BALANCE & HARMONY

Balance refers to the commitment to establishing priorities and aligning all family resources—money, time, and energy—so that your life reflects those values and priorities. It means a fair balance of power in the marriage and the family. It means that every family member has a voice in the decisions that impact his/her life, and that fairness and transparency is central to the reasoning that guides final decisions.

Harmony describes an atmosphere of peace and comfort pervading a household when all the above conditions exist. Harmony involves wanting the best for each person and encouraging each person to be the best he or she can be. It also includes having well-understood guidelines for resolving conflict; where the primary consideration is maintaining loving relationships. Unhealthy rivalry in the family is circumvented by mutual support, understanding, and cooperation, allowing for continued change in the journey, and trusting and believing in the marriage in a way that encourages risk-taking.

CONTRIBUTION

The natural outgrowth of these principles is an internal imperative to give back, to contribute to the greater good. Those who feel blessed by God are eager to pass those blessings along to others less fortunate. It is important for parents to model and instill in children an awareness and gratitude for how privileged they are, and foster an obligation to share their good fortune with others.

COMMUNITY

All of us live our lives within a larger community. Humans are social beings requiring communion with others. What follows naturally from these values is a desire to exemplify and promote these values not only in our relationships and families, but in our churches, schools, and communities.

Ways to promote these values in a healthy manner include:

- Modeling a healthy marriage in work, play, and social groups.

- Incorporating what is healthy from the Family of Origin (FOO) into the marriage/family relationship.

- Making use of church and community events and opportunities to instill a sense of community and enhance your couple and family leisure time.

PART ONE

THE FOUR COMPASS
POINTS OF MARRIAGE

Prologue

PAST, PRESENT & FUTURE: THE JOURNEY BEGINS

Why another book on improving your marriage? Hundreds of books are available, covering every possible subject on the institution of marriage; surely nothing new is left to be said. And I have read all those books in my quarter century as a practicing psychotherapist, and more than thirty years as a wife.

How can it be that even after the millions of words written on the subject, the divorce rate still stands at 50 percent, as it has for the past half-century? What will it take to reduce the failure rate of divorce when even couples of faith fail just as frequently? How can we do a better job of supporting couples and families so they will succeed?

In the process of researching, designing, and testing a program for couples, it became increasingly clear the factors for success are not a secret and haven't been for many centuries. Every sacred tradition and writing, scripture, philosopher, and sage has tried to tell us throughout the ages the secret to happy relationships. Basically, every sacred tradition reveres the same teachings when it comes to how human beings should relate to one another.

If the truth has been available to us all along, what are we missing? There must be a paradigm that frees us from our fears…of exposure, of dependency, of rejection, of failure, of vulnerability. Is there a guarantee against the perils universal to the human condition? No! Does such a formula for redemption exist? Yes!

Couples think their "stuff" is unique to them, and they deal with their "stuff" in various, but predictable ways. Most couples will have issues or conflict in some areas and not in others. Other couples have a single issue that screams so loudly they can't even connect to one another in the areas that are working properly. Some couples have gotten into the habit of battling over every little thing at one end of the spectrum, and others sweep anything uncomfortable under the rug at the other end…most fall in-between those extremes. Neither strategy provides a lasting solution.

Eventually, something or someone blows the lid off and creates a crisis. Divorce seems the sad but inevitable resolution—if not the only, at least the easiest way out—but it's not. Not for the parents, nor for the children.

Discovering a Dynamic Marriage is based on a simple concept. That's not meant to suggest that any process for creating a long-lasting relationship between human beings is easy. Simple in theory doesn't mean easy in practice. Rarely is something of value ever accomplished easily. But rewarding is another matter. Nothing in human experience is more desired and rewarding than a happy marriage and a thriving family, especially when it is undergirded by commitment to a shared spiritual practice.

You will notice an emphasis on courage and daring throughout the book. The word **DARE** was in the working title of the book, which in the end was shortened. The concept of daring—and the risk-taking it implies—however, remains a critical component of the journey. Any seagoing voyage is a risky venture, even today. An unfaltering spirit of ***discovery, daring,*** and ***determination*** are the qualities driving the journey toward a successful and ***Dynamic Marriage.***

HOW THIS BOOK IS ORGANIZED

Discovering a Dynamic Marriage is divided into five sections that define significant arenas or zones of marriage. The sections contain chapters that break down and delve into specific subjects in depth. Part I is called the Four Compass Points of Marriage for a reason. It is important to grasp the novel concept of ***Dynamic Marriage*** and begin your journey charting a clear course on these four compass points.

The captain of a ship would never set out on a sea voyage without a compass and a navigation chart. The compass points represent the key knowledge and skills to build successful relationships. Diligence is required to master the concepts and skills, but they will create the map for you to navigate each of the remaining eight areas, even those that have been highly conflicted in the past.

The book is organized as a progression through twelve specific areas of marriage. A chapter is devoted to each of these areas and explores the underlying feelings and beliefs that cause conflict and problems in that area. Each chapter seeks to promote understanding of the embedded scripts at the root of the conflict and the way to resolve it moving forward.

Each chapter introduces the concepts necessary for success in that specific area and builds the foundation for the chapters that follow. Most couples find they do well in certain areas and muddle around in others. Even couples who begin Dynamic Marriage claiming they "fight about everything" find that only a few fundamental beliefs are at the core of all their issues. Most of these beliefs do not stand up under scrutiny.

When couples examine their family-of-origin scripts, they generally laugh with relief as the comprehension dawns. Suddenly, the feelings of hopelessness evaporate and they feel in control of their future.

MEASURING PROGRESS

You may not notice your headway at any individual moment, but as new ways of thinking and behaving replace default beliefs and strategies from the past, you will gradually begin to feel the shift in yourself and your relationship. You may notice after the fact that you handled a sticky situation differently than you had in the past. Acknowledge and celebrate all the wins no matter how seemingly insignificant.

Recalling the concept of an invisible contract that underpins all relationships, each chapter's goal is to help you negotiate and draft a clause that will govern your future decisions and behaviors in each specific area of your relationship. The purpose for the Rules and Guidelines that prohibit going into past offenses and errors will become clear to you. When you understand that you "didn't know what you didn't know," and when you uncover the default behaviors that cause pain to those you love and/or that hurt you, letting go of the past, then forgiveness will follow naturally.

The family you grew up in—your family of origin (FOO)—is the classroom where you learn about relationships at an early age you can no longer remember. You will learn that these embedded "scripts" drive your relationship behaviors. These subconscious scripts or models are much more powerful than any beliefs you embrace consciously. Your goal is to choose the beliefs and behaviors that will with consistency and mutual support become your new defaults.

PART I: THE FOUR COMPASS POINTS

So let's dive into what it means in terms of locating the compass points. Imagine for a moment that you are standing on the ocean's shore. Imagine you are the captain of the ship, the person responsible for getting the ship safely across the vast sea. How would you know which direction to go? What are the markers you can use to guide the way? What could you count on to show the way across uncharted seas to an island paradise you dream exists but have never seen?

Would you be in a hurry to start sailing, or would you take as much time as required to chart the course to the dream destination? As the captain or ship builder, would you delegate this pivotal task—your life—to anyone else?

Consider this scenario as a metaphor for marriage. It's not as if you arrive at mating age without a map; it's just that it is not conscious, nor by your choice. The internal compass—

we'll be referring to it as a script, model, or map throughout the book—is already embedded in your unconscious. You literally soaked it up, piecing it together like a jigsaw puzzle, struggling to make sense of confusing adult behavior, from a child's limited and dependent perspective.

THE DISCOVERY BEGINS

So, as in the metaphor, your voyage originates with a joint decision about your destination and charting the journey's course. Only in this instance, the exploration will be into your own unique early history, buried deep in your psyche, to examine the origins of the touchstone beliefs you hold about yourself, gender, roles, marriage, and family. You will repeat this journey at the beginning of every chapter to uncover the roots of the embedded beliefs and scripts each subject contains.

Half of couples actually do succeed in making a lasting marriage; most of those who do grew up with parents who never divorced. They have a script or mental model of an enduring relationship. However, enduring does not necessarily mean healthy or happy or one you want to emulate in your own marriage.

On your journey through *Discovering a Dynamic Marriage*, you will follow the lives of several couples who illustrate the challenges of many couples who didn't have the benefit of this knowledge. In their stories, you will get to know them and identify with their challenges, failures, trials, and triumphs. Of course, the families' names have been changed to protect their identities, but their stories and struggles are real.

The series of journeys through each of the chapters is your declaration of independence. You will dredge up and examine—*Discover*—the old scripts and maps and update with the information you choose from what you are learning. Then chart your own course—*Dare*—to the relationship you desire—a *Dynamic Marriage*. You are the chart-makers, the builders, and captains of the ship.

Let the voyage begin!

OUR GOALS FOR PART 1:
THE FOUR COMPASS POINTS

SECRET #1

COMFORT & CONNECTION: COURTSHIP, ROMANCE & SEX

"Every lasting marriage goes through a series of 'divorces' in its lifetime."
— Paul Fairweather, Ph.D.

The above quotation is the best advice on marriage I ever received as a young wife and mother. The words did not sound encouraging upon first hearing them. But over the years, they came back again and again to remind me to keep "hanging in there" when plodding through the inevitable deep valleys that occur in every relationship.

The "divorces" referred to above are times of trudging through the bottom of the valley, when what was working fine for a period of time is no longer making the grade. As a couple, you repaint walls, reseed lawns, replace worn furniture, renovate outdated bathrooms, and discard obsolete appliances, but you don't seem to consider reviving diminished desire or updating outworn, ineffective relationship strategies and behaviors.

When couples finally face the truth of the emptiness they feel and the distance growing between them, they are apt to jump to the conclusion that the marriage is no longer viable. Once the mind starts down that track, the predictable path is the building of a case that supports their fears. Formerly innocuous behaviors are suddenly irritating. Comments are negatively interpreted that previously would have gone unnoticed.

The following story illustrates the discouraging deep valley passages that can exist in marriage:

Jerry and Sue Thompson came to Penny, a church marriage counselor, in their mid-thirties. They had been married for twelve years with two children. When Penny asked them why they were there, they said, "We want a Christian divorce." Penny gulped, silently prayed for wisdom, and asked how they had arrived at this decision?

"We care about each other and we want to continue to parent our children together, but we just don't love each other anymore. We want help to divorce in a Christian way, to stay friends and be good parents."

Penny found herself saying aloud, "Good!" Internally, she was saying, "Good? This is not good, this is terrible!" She continued to speak with the Thompsons. "It sounds like you have run out of love, like your car running out of gas. It's good that you know that and are able to admit it honestly to each other."

The Thompsons seemed relieved that Penny understood their feelings. She continued to talk with them and piece together the circumstances that had led to the decision to end their marriage. Near the end of the hour, she said:

"I am touched by the caring and consideration I have observed and that you have expressed for each other. I've been married for a long time and I know what it feels like to run out of love. I also know that sometimes God can fill you back up. Would you be willing to meet weekly with me for the next six weeks? You pray and I'll pray. Let's see if God will fill you up with love again. Would you be willing to delay your final decision for six weeks and see what God wants to do?"

Stunned, the couple looked at one another and slowly nodded their agreement, first to each other and then to Penny. She sat alone quietly afterwards, praying and wondering whether she had done the right thing.

Four days later, she received a phone call from an elated Sue Thompson. "He did it! He did it!"

Penny, taken by surprise, asked, "Who did what?" Sue told her that God had indeed filled them back up with love. "We're more in love than we have ever been!"

Weathering the rough seas or flat, windless days in a relationship are an inescapable part of the voyage. That is where commitment comes into play. Commitment is the navigation chart that holds you to your goals and keeps you on course to your desired destination. The ship far out to sea has no alternative but to ride out the storms and endure days on end becalmed—with no wind in the sails—no movement, no progress, no land in sight. The vows you made when you married are more like the ship at sea than a merry-go-round you can jump on and off at your whim.

Resorting to blame and justification accelerates the downward slide toward the state of hopelessness that lands a marriage in divorce court. In the majority of cases, divorce is not the best answer—not a good answer for the partners and certainly not for the children. Longitudinal studies tracking the effects of divorce on children disprove the popularly held view that children adjust. They don't! The emotional damage lasts a lifetime.[1]

Following divorce, the entire relationship path of a person's life can be forecast according to his or her age when parents' divorced. This is a wake-up call. When parents can't find a way to resolve differences, ride out storms, or stand by commitments, what have children learned about life and love?[2]

LOOKING FOR LOVE IN ALL THE WRONG PLACES

Replacing lost love is the objective at the root of most divorces, either before or after the decree. When it comes before, it is called infidelity. Most infidelity has its root in a misdirected attempt to find the excitement and passion originally felt with your beloved. Once you have experienced real love and passion, an aching void opens when it wanes and gradually disappears in the busyness of everyday life.

Like many people, you may become aware your marriage has gone flat only when you experience a sudden intense attraction to someone outside the marriage. You feel driven to fill the void and discover passion again. Infidelity is often cast as the ultimate sin within the scope of relationships. According to Christian Scripture, there is no hierarchy of sins, and the standard of conduct goes far beyond overt action:

"But I tell you that anyone who looks at a woman lustfully has already committed adultery with her in his heart."
(Matthew 5:28)

The path to infidelity is not sudden; it is marked by a series of gradual steps leading to thinking about other potential relationships, or entertaining the possibility of ending the marriage. As a broader interpretation of the warning in the verse above, the first step toward infidelity is in directing energy away from the marriage rather than doubling efforts to reconnect to your spouse. Infidelity is often referred to as "straying", and it begins with thoughts straying from keeping the beloved in first place in your mind.

Remember, thoughts are things:

"For as he thinks in his heart, so is he."
(Proverbs 23:7)

In a period of disillusionment and distress in your marriage, it is easy to lapse into the trap of faithless thinking, believing it to be harmless. But the verses above warn against allowing the mind to wander down a track that leads away from, rather than toward, the spouse to whom you have made a lifetime commitment. When you entertain thoughts in conflict with your values, your brain is gradually conditioned to accept those thoughts and set up a situation to turn them into reality. The process is called rationalization.

It is easy to forget, when yearning to recapture a loving connection, that the object of an attraction is not the source of your feelings.

The feelings are generated and expressed within you. One of the most difficult tasks in growing up—truly growing up—is learning to love yourself. When you mature to the place where you are able to release yourself from the constant quest for love, approval, and appreciation outside yourself, you are truly free.

Nothing enslaves you like the incessant need for validation. A spouse is never up to the task. Two other-referenced partners, dependent on each other for reassurance that they are valued human beings, is a recipe for failure.

A predictable consequence of the quest is an attraction to someone outside the marriage to fill the insatiable need for validation. Interpret the attraction as a warning signal that you have not been taking stock of your own inner world, or attending to the need for romance and excitement in your marriage. It's the classic cliché—"looking for love in all the wrong places."

It is not only the need that is at fault; it is the misinterpretation of where the solution lies. Looking outside rather than inside for answers is a way of abdicating responsibility for your own decisions and feelings, your own life, marriage, and family. If you are not in charge, who is? What can your spouse and family rely on if your decisions are based on shifting feelings rather than the commitments your heart has entered into?

THE ROAD TO DIVORCE

To justify what you want to do, you begin case-building and finding fault, setting your partner up as the cause of your discontent, blaming and making your spouse responsible for the dissatisfactions in the marriage. Even feelings of guilt are ascribed to your unappreciated and unacknowledged loyalty, further justifying—in your own eyes—the right to engage in irresponsible behavior. Poor victim you!

The line I hear most often from unfaithful partners is: "I've never felt like this before." Of course you haven't. You couldn't. You haven't been who you are now before now. You have learned, grown, matured, and taken on greater responsibility. Just by virtue of having made a lifetime commitment to another person, you have changed. The process of building a life with someone, learning the delicate dance of accommodation, balancing one another's needs, has taught you about the blessings of both giving and receiving.

If you have brought children into the world, you have experienced a kind of love for which you would give your life. Of course you feel different than you ever have—you are changed, deeper, more complex, more mature.

THE CONSEQUENCES

With the exception of life and death issues, the demise of a marriage may be the greatest catastrophe in a child's life. But divorce is not only a trauma for the children. The adults don't really get over it either. The sense of guilt and failure does not subside over time. As the aftershocks unfold, these feelings intensify.

As we mature and become more honest with ourselves, as we outgrow youthful bravado—being humbled and tempered by life—as we see our children making the mistakes they learned from us, we learn about regret. There may be nothing more deeply painful!

A study by a prominent magazine asked divorced people a series of questions. Did the divorce solve the problems they divorced to solve? Sadly, 85 percent answered, "No." Those who had remarried were asked whether they were working harder in the second marriage than they did in their first? The majority responded, "Yes."

Further inquiry asked if they had worked as hard in their first marriage as they were in their second, would they still be married? Again the answer was, "Yes"! When people who had experienced both divorce and a spouse's death were asked, "Which was the most painful recovery?" without hesitation, the consistent answer was "Divorce"!

The feedback I get from remarried couples in Dynamic Marriage sessions confirms the same theme. "If my first spouse and I had gone through this process, we would still be married." The tragedy voiced in this admission is heartbreaking. Even though life has gone on and they have found new love, a lifetime of needless heartache has been set in motion.

Unfortunately many [divorced parents] stay intensely angry with one another. In our study, a third of the couples were fighting at the same high pitch ten years after their divorce was final. Their enduring anger stemmed from continued feelings of hurt and humiliation, fueled by new complaints (child support is too burdensome or too little), jealousy over new, often younger partners. The notions that divorce ends the intense love/hate relationship of marriage is another myth of our times.[3]

In the long run, parents don't anticipate the deep anguish that hits years later. Adult children of divorce rarely consider their parents' subsequent homes, their home. The family circle is broken and no longer beckons them home for celebrations, holidays, and visits. Generally, adult children who stay close to their parents have parents who remained together. We refer to them as intact families. The name says it all!

I am certainly not suggesting that no legitimate reasons for divorce exist. Of course there are. Nor am I suggesting that a divorce is an unmitigated disaster that can't be mended. Again, there are many steps that can be taken to repair relationships and renew grown children's faith in love and marriage. It is your responsibility to help. The skills you will learn in these pages will show you the way.

CHANGING THE PATTERN

People change and grow over time, and for many valid reasons. You don't stop growing the day you marry. The advent of children into the home changes you as individuals and changes your relationship. Priorities are reordered, perceptions shift, your individual and marital worlds contract and expand. As you change, the relationship must adjust to meet the needs of the individual each of you has become. If you fail to acknowledge and embrace the growth, the relationship is in jeopardy.

The necessary mini-divorces referred to in the opening paragraphs don't end in court. They are wake-up calls. A time for re-evaluation. A time to remember and celebrate those things in each other and in the relationship you cherish. A time to rejoice in the love that brought you together, to build on the parts you do well, and to face honestly and with open hearts the elements that no longer serve you and let them go.

Divorcing the old relationship and making conscious choices about what you each need as individuals and as partners is the wise way to proceed as you move forward. In this first chapter, you take the first step—courtship, romance, and sex. Let's begin at the beginning.

ROMANCE REDUX

When you fell in love, you made your relationship a top priority…perhaps THE top priority. You couldn't spend enough time in the company of the object of your affection. You probably invested a great deal of time and energy planning and engaging in a variety of romantic courtship behaviors to present yourself in the best light in order to secure your beloved's affections.

A notable expert on the subject of relationships is John Welwood, author of *Love and Awakening*. In an article titled "Intimate Relationship as a Spiritual Crucible," Welwood describes love this way:

> *Falling in love ushers in a special period with its own distinctive glow and magic. Glimpsing another person's beauty and feeling our heart opening in response provides a taste of*

absolute love, a pure blend of openness and warmth. This being-to-being connection reveals pure gold at the heart of our nature—qualities like beauty, delight, awe, deep passion and kindness, generosity, tenderness, and joy.

Yet opening to another also flushes to the surface all kinds of conditioned patterns and obstacles that tend to shut this down: our deepest wounds, our grasping and desperation, our worst fears, our mistrust, our rawest emotional trigger points. As a relationship develops, we find that we don't always access the gold of our nature, for it is embedded in the base metal of conditioned patterns.[4]

Commitment changes things between lovers over time. The inescapable demands of real life begin to intrude on a couple's time and resources. The fire diminishes and the long descent into dissatisfaction, discouragement, and finally, despair ensues. Couples generally misdiagnose the signs.

The marriage, almost imperceptibly, becomes increasingly less intimate and satisfying. In growing frustration, you fall into the trap of case-building, and racking up the ways in which your spouse doesn't measure up to your expectations. You begin making assumptions about the meaning behind the feelings and behaviors you observe. You start keeping score: counting disappointments, misinterpreting the meaning of behaviors, judging, blaming, shifting responsibility… the list goes on.

A relationship takes on a life of its own. It is meant to. Marriage consists of two individuals with their own needs, feelings, fears, expectations, and baggage. What you create together is the vessel holding your shared love, hopes, aspirations, and dreams. Psychologist and relationship researcher John Gottman—famous for his "relationship labs" at the University of Washington that predict whether a couple will make it—says:

> ...for me the relationship is the unit, rather than the person. What I focus on is a very ephemeral thing, which is what happens between people when they interact. It's not either person, it's something that happens when they're together. It is like a structure that they're building by the way they interact. And I think of it that way, almost like a fleeting architectural fluid form that people are creating as they talk to each other, as they smile, as they move.[5]

Imagine your relationship as a third entity—a joint creation—a thing of substance and beauty, worthy of investment and protection. Whatever condition it is in at the present moment, you are equally responsible for it.

When you are hurt, angry, confused, and upset, you find it nearly impossible to hear one another or back down from a position you have taken. But, when either of you can remember it is the relationship you both treasure that is at stake, you can take a step back to break the stalemate and enter into a productive dialogue.

Much of what goes into the molding of your relationship vessel is a reaction to whatever you saw in your parents' marriages that you don't want to repeat. The problem is that the script invisibly embedded in your subconscious is the classroom of your parents' marriage. You don't have another model. Much of the conflict in a marriage is, at its core, ***a battle over whose dysfunctional family of origin will prevail!*** We will revisit this theme in nearly every chapter…so keep it in mind. The calamity is that rarely do either of you truly want to repeat your parents' relationship.

Instead of fighting to re-enact a model of marriage and family you don't actually want, direct your energy and resources into creating the relationships you really do want. Your personal task is to become the partner you want to have.

In a candid interview with John Welwood regarding what he learned from his own failed marriage, he speaks of "waking up in relationship" as an "heroic journey."

> *To bring consciousness to an area that has never been conscious before is an heroic journey. A conscious relationship is one that puts you completely to the test as a human being. It involves becoming clear about what we are doing with another person and what that requires of us.*

> *I didn't know the first thing about relationships actually. I had lots of ideas and images in my mind about what they should be—but I didn't know a thing about what they really take. And that's because I really didn't know all that much about myself. So the question of how to have a conscious relationship is how to be.*

> *What we most cherish with another person are the moments of just being together. Not even so much being together as being together. All the best intimate moments are those in which we are simply present—being ourselves, not having to*

*do something, not having to prove anything—simply shar-
ing that with someone we love.*

*So love inspires us to be more present. That is why we value
it so much…the strongest connection is the quality of being
they experience in each other's presence. What it's really about
is how a relationship keeps inviting us to explore how to be,
how to be who we really are.[6]*

Blissful romantic encounters are spontaneous and cannot be
manufactured. However, in a long-term relationship, such
moments don't happen at all unless the stream of affection
and appreciation out of which they flow is intentionally nurtured and choreographed into our lives and practiced daily.
Creating time and space for magic to happen doesn't guarantee that bliss will follow, but NOT making courtship gestures
and quality couple time a priority is a guarantee that magic
is unlikely to occur.

Making romantic liaisons a relationship tradition will ensure
that, from time to time, those incandescent moments will
bubble up. Expand the definition of foreplay in your marriage. It isn't something you engage in when you want to
have sex; it is the affectionate manner in which you relate to
your beloved in everyday interactions that inevitably lead to
intimate, loving encounters on a regular basis.

The first step in creating a Dynamic Marriage is a nostalgic
trip down memory lane with your beloved. This approach
assumes that if you are to build a more exciting, vibrant relationship, it should be built on a foundation of the past's most
memorable moments and experiences.

So start your journey where it began and see what you learn from it that you can carry into the future. This initiates the "Dare to Discover" part of the equation: an heroic exploration into the internal roadblocks that stand in the way of you being the partner you want to be, in the Dynamic Marriage you want to have.

EXERCISES:

Loved & Special List (L & S)

This exercise seems so simplistic it is easy to overlook it. On the contrary, it is the basis for all that follows in turning your marriage around. Don't neglect it. Use it consistently to have a profound effect on your relationship and set you on the road to the loving connection that forms the first compass point in your marriage.

Make a L & S list:

- Each of you will make a list of at least thirty things, words, or gestures that make you feel Loved & Special.

- List things your partner has done and add things you wish he or she would do.

- Exchange lists.

- The L & S list is a living, "dynamic" document that will only be effective if consistently used, expanded, and updated.

- Make a date within the next week to share your lists with each other.

Ideas to put on your L & S list:

- Favorite romantic dates, affectionate words that touched you, expressions of love, appreciation, validation, and support.

- Add new things your partner does that you really like, such as: romantic gestures, affectionate words, a juicy kiss, celebration—the possibilities are endless—make a big deal of it.

How to use your L & S list:

- Every day, choose one item from your partner's list to give as a gift. You can't go wrong if it's on the list. Have fun with it.

- Look for chances to surprise. Take risks. Be grateful. Cultivate your appetite for delight and wonder. Develop curiosity.

- If you remember nothing else…remember this: SURPRISE & CURIOSITY. These two elements that make children so charming and delightful will keep your relationship eternally exciting and juicy!

Ideal Partner:

- Make a list of all the qualities and traits you appreciate and/or would like to see in your partner.

- Being totally honest, check off those that currently apply to you.

- The ones left unchecked are the work you have to do on yourself.

- Make a separate list of the things you need to work on in order to become the partner you want to have.

Discussion Questions:

Consider and answer each question individually and then discuss your answers together.

1. What is your favorite humorous memory of something that happened when you were dating?

2. What is your favorite romantic memory since your marriage?

3. What did you do while courting that would make your marriage more fun now?

4. Think about your parents' marriage.

   a. What did you admire and hope to emulate?

   b. What did you dislike and want to avoid?

   c. In what ways have you succeeded and/or failed in either case?

5. Describe your ideal date.

6. Name three wishes for your marriage that you hope will result from reading *Discovering a Dynamic Marriage*?

7. What are three steps you can take in the next week to make that happen?

OUR AGREEMENT ON COURTSHIP, ROMANCE & SEX

VALUES & VISION:
ETHICS, GOALS & BOUNDARIES

It is not merely unfortunate but truly preposterous that most couples have never engaged in a critical sit-down dialogue about their personal values and integrity: moral, ethical, spiritual, financial, and lifestyle. During the dance of courtship, couples make a series of unverified assumptions about the behaviors, values, and beliefs of the other.

Needless to say, when dating, the primary objective is to present yourself in the best possible light. Pheromones and oxytocin are coursing through the veins and seeping out of every pore of lovers, as nature designed for the human race's perpetuation. These are the driving forces and reason is on hiatus. Courtship is a period of suspended reality, filled with illusion, denial, and hope.

By the time a relationship has progressed to commitment, each person has a sense—often misguided—that he or she understands the moral and ethical code governing the prospective partner's life. Many times, the false sense of security is further supported by membership in an organization, or allegiance to a creed whose tenets they share. In many cases, it is religion, which is a good beginning.

A mutual faith provides a solid core to build a life around, but it is only one necessary ingredient for a working set of values and moral guidelines forming the foundation for a shared life. If shared faith constituted a guarantee that a relationship would last, the marital success rate for couples of faith would be far above average. The marriage of Janet and Rafe Johnson illustrates how this breakdown between faith and values can occur.

Janet was the daughter of a minister. She was born when her father was twenty-six, married just over a year, having completed one semester of college. He made the decision to go into ministry shortly before meeting Janet's mother and began his educational pursuit. Janet was twelve when her dad finally earned his Ph.D., during which time he was employed as a pastor. She was raised with a high regard for the value of education and service to others.

In the Johnson family, money was equated with success, personal worth and status. Rafe, as the son of a highly successful "self-made" man, tended to judge people by their net worth rather than their worthiness as people. For Janet, ethical questions were black and white: ethics was more pragmatic for Rafe. In business situations, he said whatever was required to close the sale. Janet saw this as dishonest and inauthentic, which gradually eroded her respect for him. This behavior also led to doubting his trustworthiness with her.

Like his father, Rafe's first allegiance was to the business. He traveled half the time and was only marginally involved in the daily life of his young family. Janet was accustomed to a

*dad who was deeply involved in family life. In her parents'
marriage, Mom's position as the pastor's wife, and the pastor's family, was an integral part of his success. They were
all in ministry together as a team. Mom also served as the
church's wedding planner and led women's ministries and so
she had a respected role of her own.*

*Janet's valiant struggle to find a significant role in Rafe's
"real" life was continually frustrated. Although she made
huge contributions to his family's business and his success,
her central position in Rafe's life was not only unacknowledged but actively undermined by his family, particularly by
his mother.*

All legally sanctioned entities begin with a binding contract
that spells out the duties and responsibilities of the parties
involved. Every business relationship requires some kind
of financial or contractual agreement that spells out the relationship's terms and conditions. You can't even get a cell
phone or Internet connection without a contract. Without
an examination and understanding of the internal values and
scripts that drive your behavior and beliefs, you are struggling in the dark like in the Johnsons' tragic tale that eventually ended in divorce.

Marriage is a small business. When you consider the com-
bined household income of most couples, budgets, expenses,
and assets over the lifetime they will spend together, it totals
upwards of a million dollars for even middle-income families. You would not enter into any other kind of financial
partnership with anyone without negotiating beforehand the
agreement's terms and conditions.

When couples seeking therapy are asked about their shared values, they generally look at one another with a blank expression and are at a loss for a rational answer. A general sense of confusion exists around what shared values means outside of a simplistic reply about honesty, fidelity, raising healthy kids, and similar views on "things" that are important to them. These values are pretty much universal, but the Principles and Guidelines in Dynamic Marriage hold many of these and other values to a much higher standard.

Shared values and boundaries form the bedrock of a successful marriage. To institute them as a living, working document, they must be examined, discussed, negotiated, and mutually agreed upon in each of twelve areas of marriage.

APPLYING VALUES IN ALL AREAS

As you take the journey toward establishing your Dynamic Marriage agreement, make it a practice to dissect the values you hold in each area of marriage. For instance, look at "honesty." You may mutually agree that in the sexual arena that means fidelity. But does that include pornography?

In drafting the clause on money, does "honesty" permit cheating on your taxes? Is it okay to have a secret stash of funds?…to conceal purchases?…to hide raises or bonuses? On health…to hide compulsions or addictions? Remember there are sins of commission and omission—what does honesty mean in your values statement? Is your honesty value the courtroom variety, "If you don't ask, I don't tell," or is your honesty standard a commitment to transparency?

Mutual agreement on a set of values is the second of the Four Compass Points upon which a Dynamic Marriage is charted. It is the "quality control" document for your relationship and your life. In all twelve areas, it is essential to examine deeply the values each of you hold as a guiding standard of conduct for your life and view of the world. At the core of discovery is *curiosity*. When you *respect* your beloved, you are curious about the person's views and values. Learn to listen with *curiosity and intention to appreciate and understand*. Discover your partner's perspective on life and love and where it came from. Celebrate the values you agree upon. Write them down. When you encounter differences, consider it a creative challenge to come up with a mutually beneficial resolution.

At the core of discovery is curiosity. When you respect your beloved, you are curious about the person's views and values. Learn to listen with curiosity and intention to appreciate and understand. Discover your partner's perspective on life and love and where it came from. Celebrate the values you agree upon. Write them down. When you encounter differences, consider it a creative challenge to come up with a mutually beneficial resolution.

THE FINE ART OF COLLABORATION

This process offers a crucial opportunity to learn the gracious art of collaboration. The choice of words is intentional; the alternative word to collaboration is compromise, which suggests to most people the mutual demand for each to give up something of significance in order to come to an agreement that makes no one truly happy.

Collaboration is altogether different; it is the creation of something new and distinctive out of a novel way of combining existing ideas or materials. Great examples exist in every field of endeavor. For example, a pair of dancers is a fluid collaboration of two individuals moving together in creating a single work of art. In *Gift from the Sea*, Anne Morrow Lindbergh penned this lovely metaphor:

> *A good relationship has a pattern like the dance and is built on some of the same rules. The partners do not need to hold on tightly, because they move confidently in the same pattern, intricate but gay and swift and free, like a country dance of Mozart's. To touch heavily would be to arrest the pattern and freeze the movement, to check the endlessly changing beauty of its unfolding.*

> *There is no place here for the possessive clutch, the clinging arm, the heavy hand; only the barest touch in passing. Now arm in arm, now face to face, now back to back—it does not matter which. Because they know they are partners moving to the same rhythm, creating a pattern together and being invisibly nourished by it* [1]

Consider a team of writers who create a screenplay for a television series by combining ideas and visions, or a crew of steelworkers who work together to build a bridge connecting land to land to serve a community. Perhaps it's a team of horticulturists who fashion an arboretum from an abandoned quarry that becomes home to birds and bees, ladybugs and hummingbirds, and that astonishes children and parents with wonder at the movement and color and beauty.

Think of your Agreement as a living document, not a paper to sign and stow. In *Discovering a Dynamic Marriage*, you will master the fine art of collaboration, a spiritual practice to enrich your marriage for a lifetime.

FIDELITY

When we speak of fidelity or faithfulness, we immediately assume the subject is referring to sexual fidelity as in monogamy. Certainly, fidelity has been a primary concern of couples throughout history. But even in Western culture, the demand for fidelity applied primarily to women, who were considered property until the last century. Unfaithful wives were blamed and punished, often executed, if they strayed from the marriage bed.

The practice of fidelity was an understandable concern in the centuries before birth control. Men liked to ensure that the offspring bearing their surname were actually their progeny. In the past half-century, advances have been made in the pursuit of equality for women, and the demand for true intimacy in marriage. The notion of faithfulness has taken hold for good reasons—the rewards of shared intimacy and passion in marriage are immeasurable.

We touched on this matter previously, but it is so crucial it bears further discussion in this section on values. An extramarital affair is often a misdirected attempt to replace the excitement and magic of newfound love. To neglect the romantic and sexual dimension of your relationship until there is a crisis is all too common and tragic.

Remember, the object of attraction is not the source of your feelings. The feelings are within you. You have not been attending to the need for romance and excitement in your relationship. "Looking for love in all the wrong places," is the standard fix. The right decision is to share your loneliness and longing with your partner, to ask for help in recovering what has been lost, and to initiate growing together to the next level of loving.

The other path leads to justifying what you want to do by minimizing and undermining what is good in your marriage. Recall the familiar line from unfaithful partners, "I've never felt like this before." You never push the boundaries of your own emotional depths until your relationship demands it of you. Embrace the challenge rather than looking for a solution outside the marriage.

HONESTY

We briefly discussed the concept of honesty in the introduction, but honesty is always at the top of the list when a couple initiates a discussion of values. Honesty is a necessary condition for a profoundly intimate relationship that is dependent upon a deep level of mutual trust.

This discussion is probably not what you are expecting; it may take you to an entirely new concept of being honest with yourself and your beloved. Remember, the most basic rules of love and relationship were laid down in the Bible and in all other sacred traditions:

> *"Do unto others as you would have them do unto you,"*

and,

"Love your neighbor as yourself!"[2]

If you were able to follow these simple commands to the letter, you wouldn't need much else to maintain the highest level of honesty or any other values in every area of life. However, neither simplicity nor continuity is the reality of the human condition.

Honesty is actually a cluster of elements that make up the entire concept. Let's consider the elements one at a time. Think of them as personal character principles to which you aspire and commit rather than an intellectual exercise.

TRUST

The following principles are integral elements of being faithful, honest, and trustworthy as a person and a partner.

A deep level of emotional connection requires safety built on trust. Even loving and well-intentioned couples under stress may speak or behave in hurtful ways that damage the trust between them. When anger or stress is used as an excuse for being hurtful or insensitive, you are unfaithful and untrustworthy—to yourself, your marriage, and God's command.

Blaming another for your inability to control your behavior is irresponsible. You are always held accountable for how you choose to respond under adverse circumstances. It is the hallmark of a trustworthy adult, a well-differentiated[3] person, to accept full responsibility for the consequences and repercussions of choices and actions.

FAIRNESS

Trust requires an underpinning of fairness, one of the first concepts children understand. A toddler will howl with outrage when another child takes his toy, staking his claim, "I had it first; that's not fair!" True? Yes, but let's look at the reason behind it. Children are aware of their utter dependence on their primary caretakers for their very survival. Yes, those are the stakes.

If someone doesn't fall in love with me, make a commitment to me, and put my needs first, I'm going to die. Life or death... those are the stakes. *If I can't trust you to keep your commitment to me, I'm not safe.*

The decision to allow a beloved to become so important to you that if he or she betrays you or leaves you, you feel as if you are going to die, requires trust. The willingness to become dependent on another to meet your need for connection assumes trust. The idea that we outgrow dependency needs is a fallacy. Autonomy, not independence, is the mark of maturity. Autonomy is the goal. Independence is an illusion; it is a form of denial and denial is self-deception. Living a high standard of honesty in your relationships requires being honest with yourself first.

CRAZY-MAKING

What is crazy-making? In more intellectual terms, this behavior is called dissembling[4], but in this context, let's call it what it feels like—crazy-making. It occurs when a partner accurately senses or intuits something amiss in the energetic field of the other and asks a question like, "What's going on?" or

"Is everything okay?" Intuition is a proven scientific fact, not fantasy. We won't pursue that discussion in depth here. But our dialogue requires an acknowledgment that we human beings have the ability to pick up on others' moods, resistance, and emotional states even when elusive or unspoken.

When subtle emotional states are denied, they are toxic. Denial can be as simple a response from the partner as, "Oh, it's nothing," or "fine," or….Variations on avoidance tactics are endless and at first glance appear to be relatively benign white lies. But do they pass the trust test? Are such responses honest, or fair?

Letting your beloved feel like maybe he or she is crazy is a crucial part of the fairness concept and takes honesty to an entirely new level. It happens all the time in relationships, and because it is so subtle and difficult to pinpoint, it is rarely singled out as a betrayal of trust, but it is among the most devious.

What is the effect on the inquirer? The sensitive spouse picks up on something, and because (s)he cares, asks the question. The spouse denies/avoids/stonewalls, and the inquiring partner is left feeling confused, unsettled, and in a double bind: *Do I trust my partner or my intuition?* The other possibility is that the spouse does have a secret he or she is not willing to share, and by withholding, engenders anxiety and fear. Neither alternative is honest nor fair. It is crazy-making!

How do you deal with this situation in a way that is healthy, honest, and fair when there is a matter you are unwilling to talk about? Admit there is something on your mind and that you need to sort it out on your own before being prepared to share it. The considerate course is to include some reassurance that it has to do with a concern other than the relationship, and there is nothing to worry about.

However, if what's troubling you is a marital issue or a matter that concerns your partner, there is another rule on the fairness and honesty spectrum…read on.

TRANSPARENCY

While self-awareness is the journey into oneself, transparency is the willingness to be intimately revealed and shared with another. What does transparency look like? It involves inviting the beloved into your inner world and revealing your fears, your dreams, your wounds, your hopes, your faults, your failures, and your inadequacies. The only way to ever know you are truly unconditionally loved is to take the risk of becoming transparent and discover whether you are accepted beyond your public persona…as you really are. Of course, you have to know yourself before you can be transparent to another.

The only way to ever know you are truly unconditionally loved is to take the risk of becoming transparent and discover whether you are accepted beyond your public persona…as you really are. Of course, you have to know yourself before you can be transparent to another.

It is important to understand in this discussion that transparency is not something that one can demand from a beloved. It is not a club to force another to disclose beyond what is comfortable for them, or to judge when they choose not to disclose. Transparency is a gift…always, and only given by well-differentiated partners in an environment of safety and security.

Entering into this depth of relationship is life-altering and leads to freedom. Freedom is a word that is thrown around frequently in many contexts. But becoming a person who is transparent to yourself and your beloved is a journey into a depth of authenticity that pervades every area of life.

SECRETS VS. PERSONAL PRIVACY

Universal questions among couples are: Do I have to give up all privacy to be in a committed relationship? Does my spouse have to know everything in my mind? The answer is "No!" If not, then what is the line between personal privacy and a secret? Secrets set up a toxic spiral that destroys relationships. Secrets are crazy-making and trust-destroying. Secrets have energy that transmits to everyone in the household, but when the unsettled feeling can't be named, a spouse or child's tendency is to fault him- or herself and turn the blame inward. It is the option that provides a sense of control and reduces anxiety.

Secrets set up a toxic spiral that destroys relationships. Secrets are crazy-making and trust-destroying. Secrets have energy that transmits to everyone in the household, but when the unsettled feeling can't be named, a spouse or child's tendency is to fault herself and turn the blame inward. It is the option that at the time provides an illusion of control and reduces anxiety. In the longterm it leaves a legacy of self-doubt and shame that is difficult to identify and eradicate.

Here's a simple rule identifying the fine line between keeping a secret and the right to personal privacy. It has two guidelines, both having to do with *fairness* and *honesty*—and the Golden Rule!

1. *If the roles were reversed, would I want to know? If the* *honest* *answer is yes, what is the* *fair* *thing to* do?
   Very often the reason you want to keep something secret is because you anticipate a negative reaction and want to avoid interference or confrontation. The oft-abused rationalization is, "I just wanted to protect you." That is not personal privacy, nor kindness; that is manipulating the other out of having a voice, in the service of self-interest.

2. *Will any decision on the matter under consideration* *have an impact on my beloved's life, happiness, security,* *or well-being? If the* *honest* *answer is yes, what is the* *fair* *thing to do?*
   A marriage is a legal partnership. In a legal partnership, none of the partners is permitted to make unilateral decisions without the approval of the other partners. Once again, the "golden rule" is the standard for honesty and fairness. Ask yourself: If my partner were weighing this decision, would I want to have input? If the *honest* answer is yes, what is the *fair* thing to do? In any decision that impacts your partner's life, (s)he has a right to be a part of the decision-making process...sooner rather than later.

In any decision that impacts your partner's life, (s)he has a right to be a part of the decision-making process...sooner rather than later.

SAFETY & SECURITY

When a partner violates the safety and/or trust of a beloved, it sows seeds of doubt and promotes self-protection. In self-protection, the heart closes in and seeks to defend itself. Dan Allender makes the following statement in *Bold Love*:[5]

> *The choice to love, with the inherent confusion, risk and uncertainty, is forsaken for the relative safety of self-protection. Self-protection is the self-centered commitment to act without courage, compassion, boldness, and tenderness for the sake of the other.*

I would add *humility* to Allender's list. Humility! The success of all Twelve-Step programs like Alcoholics Anonymous begins with a confession of powerlessness. The dreaded and powerful Fourth Step requires a "fearless moral inventory." The road to salvation begins with confession of sin. The road to an intimate relationship requires honest self-assessment, self-knowledge, and *humility*,"[6] and revealing your imperfect self to a beloved. Self-protection is the enemy of personal growth, integrity, and therefore, of loving relationships.

The road to an intimate relationship requires honest self-assessment, self-knowledge, and humility,"[7] and revealing your imperfect self to a beloved. Self-protection is the enemy of personal growth, integrity, and therefore, of loving relationships.[7]

AUTONOMY, COMPETENCE, & SELF-AWARENESS

Healthy adults need to feel they are capable and competent in their careers and in their relationships.

Courageous pursuit of self-awareness is the first step in your growth toward autonomy, competence, authenticity, and capacity for intimacy. You cannot give to another what you are unable to give to yourself. You cannot ask of another what you will not ask of yourself. You cannot encourage others to go where you refuse to go. You will not get honesty from others until you are scrupulously honest with yourself. And honesty takes courage because it involves risk.

The default path of self-protection is a commitment to self-deception, to denial, to self-sabotage and to superficial relationships. When you choose to deny your wounds, your faults, your fears, your losses and your longings, you require those around you to be a party to the deception. Recall the child's tale of "The Emperor's New Clothes."[8] The only person deceived was the emperor himself. This snare is one of self-protection and self-deception—the only person deceived is yourself. You can't have an open-hearted, transparent relationship in the presence of self-protection and self-deception.[9]

This snare is one of self-protection and self-deception—the only person deceived is yourself. You can't have an open-hearted, transparent relationship in the presence of self-protection and self-deception.[10]

INTEGRITY

The emotional environment required for a highly evolved degree of intimacy demands a commitment to honesty far beyond mere truth-telling. It begins with a deep vow of truth with yourself: to grow up, to face your woundedness, your losses and longings, to confront your insecurities, to complete the work of differentiation, and to acknowledge self-deception.

In other words, the path to becoming a partner with integrity, who is capable of a genuine relationship. The rewards for engaging in this work is a transcendent marriage—the kind of integrity, the kind of life, and the kind of marriage God promises those who "love one another as [The Creator] loves us."

MONEY

Secret #9 is completely devoted to negotiating an agreement on handling money. But in this discussion of values, it is crucial to come to a shared understanding of your values and the *meaning* of money. What does it represent to each of you? Power, prestige, control, status, superiority, security? Is it a means to an end or an end in itself?

How important are money and material things to each of you? How much of your time and energy are you willing to invest in acquiring money and stuff? What are you willing to give up now for security later? In the history of the natural world, only humans take more than they need to live. Only humans hoard things they don't need to the deprivation of others. An ancient wise man wrote:

Money is simply a currency representing energy. Like a river it flows along bringing life wherever it goes. Take what you need and allow it to flow on to the next person who needs it. It will be flowing by still on the morrow.[9]

ROBUST & SATISFYING SEX

A vibrant sex life is designed to be an exclusive intimate act, an expression of love for your beloved. Most other needs can be met in other ways, but sexual connection is exclusive. The term *intimacy* is most often assumed to be a reference to sex. Sex, however, can be anything but intimate. In fact, sex can become a substitute for real intimacy.

Sex is not the most intimate activity in which couples engage; communication with transparency is. Self-revelation, entrusting your fears, doubts, and wounds to the beloved… that is true intimacy. When a deep level of trust and transparency exist between partners, rare moments of connection transcending human understanding are bestowed upon us. These precious moments are the closest we as humans ever come to an experience of Divine Love.

David Schnarch[11] views sex as a barometer for the health of a relationship. Each partner honestly needs to express his or her feelings in regards to how much sex is a priority. It is not necessary to have the same ranking of priorities; most couples don't. Sex is one of those areas where it is paramount to negotiate an agreement, taking both partners' healthy and reasonable sexual appetites and desires into account. Repressed dissatisfaction with your sex life is insidious, like a cancer.

In the twenty-first century, we continue to raise our male children differently than females. At an age when boys still have strong dependency needs for comfort and connection, society makes demands in various ways that they "man-up." As a society, we have idealized the caricature of desirable males as insatiable sexual animals. Research shows that well-differentiated males have an entire repertoire of satisfying ways to establish and maintain connection. Today, we know that sexual appetites in self-referenced males and females are not all that different. You will become better acquainted with this terminology in the next chapter.

Today, we know that sexual appetites in self-referenced males and females are not all that different. You will become well-acquainted with this terminology in the next chapter.

In many cases, an adult's preoccupation with sex and/ or unbridled sexual behavior signals unexamined child-hood attachment[12] wounds and unmet dependency needs. Unsatisfied nurturance needs may get translated into insatiable sexual demands in adulthood that can become compulsive. Such behavior is a distorted attempt to feel connected, and it works only for the moment. But since it doesn't address the underlying wounds, it is not a lasting solution and may become an obsession.

There is a sense urgency to this type of sexual activity that has an uncomfortable edge. It conceals an unspoken and/unconscious agenda that feels false and eventually dampens a partner's enthusiasm. This situation results in what may be inaccurately interpreted as unequal sexual appetites. Our society idealizes a high sex drive and is too quick to misdiagnose the partner with the lower sexual appetite as the problem. When sexual dissatisfaction exists in a marriage, rarely is one partner to blame; it is a multi-dimensional relationship issue.

Our society idealizes a high sex drive and is too quick to misdiagnose the partner with the lower sexual appetite as the problem. When sexual dissatisfaction exists in a marriage, rarely is one partner to blame; it is a multi-dimensional relationship issue.

A candid discussion regarding the subject of sex needs to be included in your Values agreement. It is appropriate for vibrant sexual intimacy to be high on the list of a couple's priorities and values…and for an active sex life to be a goal stretching into the future. The rise in life expectancy and vigor into the eighties includes sexual activity for couples who make it a priority and pay attention to their physical health and emotional connection.

THE ROAD FROM HERE

In drafting your Values Compass Point of your agreement, you must make an accounting of some of the common issues, roadblocks, and other considerations for your relationship. As you work your way through all twelve clauses in your agreement, Values will serve as your standards of conduct, both within yourself and in relationship to one another.

As you collaborate in each area, expect discussions to surface that require a clarification of values. Mutual agreement in an area includes clearly articulating how you agree to conduct yourself in this specific area of your relationship moving forward.

If the Values clause of the agreement is to have any real power, mutual accountability is key to its success. One of the rules you will need to adopt is a pact that each partner is responsible to point out agreement violations. Explore together what form accountability will take.

Most importantly, regarding sensitive issues or violations to the agreement, discuss how each of you can be approached or receive feedback in a manner that allows you to stay in an Open Heart place. Obviously, the first requirement is for the initiator to come from an Open Heart place.

EXERCISES

1. Each of you individually reflect on the sub-headings in the chapter and write down your own feelings and values you hold under each sub-heading.

2. Then share what you have written, allowing one another to share completely his or her thoughts on a subject before responding.

3. Listen with the heart…not formulating your response, but moving your heart into your partner's heart space in order to understand your partner better.[12]

4. This is a collaboration, not a contest. There are no correct answers.

Discussion Questions:

Collaborate on working definitions for each of the following:

- Honesty

- Fidelity

- Safety & Security

- Trustworthiness

- Transparency

- Autonomy vs. Dependency

- Privacy vs. Secrets

- Sexual Health

OUR AGREEMENT ON VALUES & VISION

Secret #3

PARTNERSHIP & COLLABORATION: POWER & CONTROL

Partnership: an association of persons joined as partners; joint interest; mutual participation.

Collaboration: a desired result created with teamwork: *A dictionary is a collaboration of experts from many fields.*

Collaborate: to work with one another, willingly cooperate, as on a specific project: *They collaborated on a screenplay.*

The dictionary definitions help clarify why a working partnership and collaboration are primary goals in a Dynamic Marriage. As marital partners and/or parents, a multitude of large and small decisions are required. Establishing a working Partnership and Collaboration allows you to make decisions more easily and consistently, and moves you toward your final cornerstone in Secret #4: Harmony & Accord, the emotional climate that enables everyone in the family to thrive.

In Secret #1, you and your partner Connected to your love story. In Secret #2, you agreed on Values and Boundaries together. Secret #3 is the cornerstone on which you master the concepts and skills of Partnership and Collaboration.

In many instances of conflict in a marriage, very little may have to do with differences and issues, but with other factors. The emotional strategies that most frequently undermine working together as partners are avoidance, arguing, and/or controlling…none of which are effective or promote Harmony and Accord.

CLEARING THE PATH

The single most pervasive and destructive dysfunction in a marriage is the struggle for power and control. Power and control issues complicate and escalate conflict in any dispute, no matter what the subject under discussion. If you are engaged in an unresolved power struggle, it is the overriding relationship roadblock and makes it virtually impossible to address any issue with clarity or objectivity.

When you understand and eliminate power and control issues from your relationship, you have the ability to turn conflict into communication.

In this chapter, you will learn how striving for power and control destroy what you want to preserve, where you learned this behavior, how society reinforces it, how the power/control spectrum operates in a relationship, and how it contaminates communication. When you have learned how to uncover and interpret the backstory,[1] you are prepared to learn how to interrupt a destructive cycle and get back on track.

In this section, you will learn to:

- Identify default power and control when they show up.

- Trace power and control behaviors to root beliefs.

- Understand fears and insecurities that make you feel vulnerable.

- Choose alternative behaviors that promote good communication.

- Enlist the support of your partner in making changes.

- Together adopt an effective process for collaboratively working your way through the knotty stuff toward the same goal: a dynamic marriage and a peaceful, nurturing home environment.

UNDERSTANDING DEFAULTS

How do avoidance, arguing, and power/control become default strategies for dealing with conflict? You come into adulthood with long-forgotten, unresolved feelings of helplessness. Everyone reverts to the emotional level of a three-year-old when scared, rejected, lonely, helpless, or discouraged.

As a child, you entertained some variation of the fantasy that somehow, if you had the power to control the people and circumstances that matter, you would never suffer or feel helpless again.

It is a given in the human condition that your life and psyche is riddled with loss and longing. You may call them by different names, but it all boils down to loss and longing. Neither you nor anybody else got all the love and attention you craved as a child. Children are insatiable for assurances of love and acceptance. They also give the unconditional love they want to receive.

Children don't keep score unless someone teaches them to. Children are not ashamed of needs, longings, or grief until they are taught to be. At some point, children embrace the myth that power and control will insulate them from loss and longing.

As an adult, when your connection with your beloved is threatened, it triggers the long-buried dependency fears of childhood. Power fantasies linger as a subliminal belief that if you were powerful (like your parents), you could make the world revolve according to your will. This belief becomes your default position when your relationship is under stress. Whatever subject is under discussion may be sabotaged by the need to win.

Until the dynamic is understood by partners, and they make a commitment to partnership and collaboration, maladaptive strategies will continue to undermine effective communication. Take a look at how default strategies develop.

SIBLING RIVALRY

Coping strategies are learned very early, at whatever age a child first encounters competition for his or her mother's attention. The strategies often begin with the birth of a younger sibling. The first ninety days is the normal intense bonding period between infant and mother. Regardless how mindful mother is of the threat to the older sibling, the child will sometimes feel neglected and displaced. So begins a pattern of competition for mother's attention, the roots of which are buried, but the emotional climate for rivalry is set up.

Children are ever vigilant for ways to deal with their fears and helplessness. The objective of a child's rivalry-motivated manipulation is to feel safe, which is secured by being the favorite child, the Top Gun. Everyone always wants to be at the top of the food chain—that's the safety zone.

Sibling rivalry is a potent way to control parents and feel powerful. Most parents fall prey to the variety of ingenious schemes children devise, inadvertently reinforcing devious behaviors by responding as the child intends. A busy parent does not have the time and energy to recognize all the ways kids play out this competitive drama.

MANIPULATION AND POWER

Children quickly discover parents are susceptible to the accusation of showing favoritism and will bend over backwards to prove otherwise. Usually, that consists of giving into the child's demands. Children learn to set-up siblings to look bad, for reprimands, for punishment.

Siblings collude to create chaos to garner a parent's attention, and then blame it on each other. The game is called "uproar." Parents generally get sucked into the uproar game by being set-up to figure out who started it…as the children intend, and the parents lose. But when parents lose...everyone loses. There are neither winners nor losers in families. They are all in the same boat and they float or sink together.

"No one wins unless everyone wins!"

Children have, as their first priority, to prove they are the favored child. This behavior is in the primitive human DNA as a survival strategy. Unfortunately, this behavior is generally tolerated by parents and caretakers as harmless, an annoying developmental stage that will be outgrown. But there is nothing harmless about sibling rivalry, and it isn't outgrown—in fact, it is adopted over time as a maladaptive relationship strategy with far-reaching, negative effects.

When the need to be constantly reassured of being the best, the favorite, top-of-the-heap is embedded as the bedrock of a person's primary belief system, it gives rise to character traits that make for troubled relationships and chronic discontent.

Manipulation played out in sibling rivalry teaches that dishonesty, competition, and winning at the expense of another is effective and rewarding. As with most illegitimate uses of power, rivalry manipulation backfires in the long run when it gets embedded as a template for relationships. If allowed to flourish, it sets up a whole cluster of disturbing beliefs and behaviors that disrupt maturation and undermine truly supportive relationships for a lifetime.

Sibling rivalry is based on a belief system that goodness—however defined in a given situation; whether love, approval, or material things—is in limited supply. If someone else gets a piece of it, there is less for you. Harboring that belief into adolescence and adult relationships has horrific consequences. In life it shows up as competiveness, grandiosity and greed.

EFFECTS OF SIBLING RIVALRY

Do you identify with any of the symptoms on this list: envy, jealousy, incessantly comparing yourself to others and coming up short, finding secret satisfaction with others' faults or fiascoes, difficulty celebrating others' successes, feeling better about yourself when others fail, finding fault with others in order to feel superior?

Are you left feeling guilty for entertaining such contemptible thoughts?

Even with those you love and whose success you sincerely support, these insidious demons nag at you, making you feel like a fraud and even more unworthy. The feelings are unrelenting and exhausting, and there seems to be no exit strategy.

You feel all the more worthless and driven to control your environment to stave off your anxiety and self-doubt. This background explains how and why the silent engine driving power and control is rooted in sibling rivalry.

THE ANATOMY OF CONFLICT

Noted psychologist and researcher John Gottman identifies four behavioral strategies that predict a marriage's demise. He dubs them the "Four Horsemen of the Apocalypse."[2] All of them are power tactics designed to control interactions that stir up unresolved childhood anxieties and fears, many of which spring from sibling rivalry.

The following list includes typical root causes and how they are used to control. Most of them can fit into any of the strategies depending on how they are employed.

- Criticism: *comes out of a need to bolster one's own self-esteem by de-valuing the other.*

- Defensiveness: *comes out of a childhood belief that you have to be perfect to be loved. So anyone pointing out a fault has to be convinced that he or she is wrong.*

- Contempt: *dismissal of the partner's thoughts, ideas, opinions, and feelings, i.e. eye-rolling, talking down, making fun of...*

- Stonewalling: *refusing to engage; may or may not include actually leaving the scene.*

AVOIDANCE

Avoidance can be learned in a variety of ways. In some families, conflict is not acknowledged or tolerated. Parents either never disagree or take conflict behind closed doors. Both behaviors teach that conflict is forbidden or dangerous.

At the other extreme, parents battle all the time and nothing ever gets resolved, so children learn that conflict causes chaos and doesn't accomplish anything. Or, children learn by experience that it is not safe to confront or disagree with their parents, or that they can never win or even get a fair hearing.

Coming into a relationship with an embedded avoidance script may result in any of the four dangerous relationship behaviors above. Stonewalling may be perceived as the extreme end of passive avoidance, but it is actually a power play. It can be played out as emotional withdrawal, sexual withholding, refusal to engage, or leaving the scene—sometimes referred to as "doorknob power."

A person who actually leaves the premises and cuts off communication for an indeterminate period is controlling. Generally, it is the partner who is not the primary caretaker of the children and household who has the option to exercise this tactic. The partner trapped at home without a voice feels angry, abused, abandoned, stuck, and frightened. The Fair and Honest Rule has certainly been violated!

Because these tactics are effective in controlling the anxiety that conflict triggers, it is difficult to give up. If you don't explore the roots of avoidance and withdrawal in your history, your marriage will not grow. If you persist in the default pattern, it will eventually destroy the relationship. Nothing in Nature stands still. Every living thing is either growing or dying.

ARGUING VS. SOLUTION-FOCUSED DISCUSSION

When couples argue and bicker, they are colluding in creating a smokescreen both to vent and to camouflage chronic dissatisfaction with the relationship. When couples engage in this dysfunctional manner, there are generally several fundamental realities identified in familiar terms:

- Red herring: whatever subject the argument appears to be about—it isn't.

- Smokescreen: one or both partners are irritated about something they are avoiding or not willing to address so they attempt to relieve tension by diverting attention from the real issues.

- Stalemate: since the argument is not about the real feelings going on between the partners, nothing ever gets resolved.

- Tuning out: neither partner is really listening because both know the whole interaction is an exercise in futility.

- Hopelessness: neither partner is listening with curiosity and intention to understand—that is, problem-solving from an Open Heart stance.

- Chronic discontent: Bickering is a seemingly benign version of this syndrome—but equally deadly. Couples constantly peck at each other like old hens in a hen house. There is no identifiable subject of the disagreement, just an incessant expression of mild displeasure, but there is probably considerable hostility beneath the facade. If you have ever spent time around a couple who habitually engage in this manner, it is miserable to be around their scarcely veiled misery.

One expected development in committed relationships is a list of recurrent issues that never seem to be resolved. When they surface in couples who engage in unproductive arguments with power and control tactics, they run a predictable course and end in a stalemate again and again. Healthy couples in a relationship with equality and mutual respect may disagree and eventually work things out.

However, the objective in Dynamic Marriage is to reduce conflict by clearing the relational playing field and replacing it with effective communication and negotiation skills.

THE CHAMPION OF HOPE

Battleground issues, as long as they keep coming up, may indicate that at least one partner has not given up hope that the couple's troubles can be resolved. In many couples, the person who refuses to walk away from difficult subjects is treated with irritation or dismissal by the other.

The spouse, who feels intuitively that danger and death lurk in the dark corner of unresolved conflict and persists in bringing it into the light of day, is often cast in an unfavorable light by the partner. But the motivation may be that he or she harbors a hope that reconciliation and intimacy can be restored.

Seen in this light, the partner who perseveres in championing for growth in the relationship, in the face of opposition, is a real hero.

But even hope demands care and feeding. If the spouse who is more motivated by fear than love continues to resist, the beloved's hopes gradually erode. When the champion's gift is interpreted as a fault by the partner, it is the saddest type of rejection.

When the champion finally gives up hope, the diagnosis is most likely terminal.

The hopeful partner cannot bear to live as hostage to fear, and the fearful spouse cannot live without the promise of freedom from fear. The fear-driven spouse unknowingly depends upon the optimistic spouse to keep hope alive without awareness that hope is a limited resource when it is imported from a source outside oneself.

When the well runs dry, the once-cheerful spouse withdraws in order to safeguard proof of life. If he or she waits too long, they are both in danger of drowning in depression and despair. Sooner or later, one or the other will find another to love and/or opt out—before or after the divorce.

THE POWER & CONTROL SPECTRUM

When the stakes are low or the subject matter inconsequential, the power/control factor is low-key, evasive, and subtle. But even when the underlying power play is subtle, it feels devious and manipulative, and it undermines trust.

As the stakes increase and the ego kicks in, the power/control factor escalates, often beginning as an argument, then verbal assault, then intensifying to intimidation and threats. One of the partners may resort to "doorknob power"; when frustration reaches an intolerable level, he or she simply leaves the scene.

If allowed to escalate, rage may become the strategy of choice, and an effective one it is for maintaining control. However, control and connection are mutually exclusive. Rage (aggression) or withdrawal (passive) only needs to occur a couple of times before the other partner learns to back down, avoiding the tipping point.

That's how power and control work—whatever it takes to get what you want in the moment regardless of the long-term collateral damage. It's a pretty good definition of selfishness and immaturity, isn't it?

At the far end of the power and control spectrum, physical violence results where the physically stronger of the pair resorts to threats or actual bodily harm to enforce his or her will on the other.

All of the above constitute violence within the definition of Dynamic Marriage—any attitude or behavior that threatens, intimidates, or engenders fear, creates distance and destroys trust.

Anything that undermines trust and intimacy in a relationship causes psychic injury, and is, therefore, by definition, a violent act.

If these behaviors are allowed to continue, it spells the slow diminishing of passion and connection. A relationship is a living thing, and as such, is subject to the same rules as all living things—it is growing or it is dying—those are the only options. Nothing in Nature stands still.

MOST FREQUENT CONFLICTS

Every relationship has its own intractable issues, but those identified as the most frequent areas of persistent conflict are:

Sex (Four Compass Points: Secret #1)

Money (Riches & Resources: Secret #9)

Parenting (Extended Family: Secret #11)

In-Laws (Extended Family: Secret #12)

Forced-choice decisions present the most challenging type of conflict. Forced-choice, as the name implies, triggers a power struggle because your partner's position blocks what you want—and vice versa. In other words, the two desires are mutually exclusive. In a power struggle, one or both partners resort to emotional blackmail—such as walking out or rage—that stops any attempt at resolution.

The Bachs, who recently celebrated their forty-fourth anniversary, love to tell this story that occurred two years into their marriage. It is a simplistic illustration of this point.

> *Bill had received a promotion on his job that meant a welcome increase in his paycheck. In addition, their annual tax refund was considerably more than they anticipated. Bill was excited and making plans to spend the windfall on a travel trailer. Kay loved the idea of a travel trailer, but on a practical level, she did not enjoy juggling a toddler on her dreaded weekly visits to the Laundromat.*
>
> *She proposed they spend the windfall on a washer and dryer. Fortunately, this option made sense to Bill. The travel trailer*

was a luxury item; the washer and dryer were essentials. Bill listened with understanding and allowed himself to be influenced by his wife's practical needs.

In forced-choice decisions, you must reach agreement because it requires participation from both of you; there is not an option to "agree to disagree." Roles, chores, earning power, career choices, division of labor, and parenting issues often fall in this category. When you take opposing positions and defend them no matter what, you are unable to put the good of the relationship first. Forced-choice decisions can cause both of you to feel that your self-worth and integrity are at stake.

SUCCESSFULLY NAVIGATING TURBULENT WATERS

You can't have intimacy as a couple without autonomy as individuals, and you can't have either in the context of an emotional battleground. The fact that you and your partner feel alienated, angry, rejected, and unappreciated does not demonstrate emotional autonomy. On the contrary, it more likely suggests that you and your partner are enmeshed or fused.

Fusion is often interpreted as intimacy, but it is not. Fusion means that each of you is dependent on the other's approval for feelings of self-worth. It is an indication that you are other-referenced rather than self-referenced. In the heat of battle, the need to be right, maintain control, and not give in are more important at that moment than your beloved or the relationship.

The original issue's subject becomes lost once the battle is engaged. Then it's all about power: who's going to prevail, who has the final word, saving face, etc. Power issues involve both partners being dependent for their sense of self on positive validation from each other. You will be unable to resolve any recurring issue until you each identify the fears, beliefs, and role models underlying power struggles and address them head-on.

Self-referencing individuals are able to stay grounded in their own okay-ness, even when they feel alienated or at odds with their spouse. They are able to put their egos aside in favor of the relationship values they agreed to when their best selves were at the helm. They are able to stay in an Open Heart place in the midst of the battleground. Even when triggered, they respond by conscious choice rather than react from a default position.

VARIOUS TREATMENT APPROACHES

Some marital treatment theories suggest that you and your partner soothe each other and make each other feel valued. This approach is referred to as "co-regulation." The goal, silent or voiced, is "peace at any price" and all will be fine. This may entail denying that you and your partner are angry and alienated. For example, when one partner is highly emotional, the other powers down to maintain balance. If one partner withdraws, the other pursues. If one partner gets angry, the other soothes. In practice if the roles went back and forth equally between partners, it might actually work to regulate and balance the relationship and be a viable system.

In reality, couples tend to adopt one role or the other and get stuck there. It becomes another version of a power struggle and has the same tactical goal as rage. When the emotional partner feels like he or she is losing, that person will escalate the emotional state until the other partner backs off to restore peace. The usual end result is control on one side and repression on the other, and the system becomes increasingly unbalanced and unfair. It is not a system that operates on the principle that no one wins unless everyone wins. It is not honest nor fair.

Another model promotes going into the past and clearing out all past hurts and grievances in a controlled professional setting. It encourages exposing all the suppressed anger and hurts at past offenses, even if it means raging at the other. The spouse on the hot seat is supported to protect him or herself emotionally and learn to listen to a partner's pain without taking it personally.

Certainly long pent-up anger can be toxic, but even a secure individual may have difficulty feeling like a worthwhile human being confronted with a laundry list of past faults and infractions. This model has been popular and effective for many couples over many years.

But in my view, there is a danger of promoting blame and self-indulgence rather than taking responsibility for your own emotional life. Hurtful words cause damage and cannot be taken back or un-remembered. When couples discover the embedded scripts that determined hurtful behavior, they find it easy to forgive and forget. You don't know what you don't know.

Self-referencing approaches teach the need to become emotionally autonomous in order to achieve a high level of intimacy and integration. You learn to modulate your own uncomfortable or destructive emotional states, soothe your own ruffled feathers, manage your own frustration, calm yourself down, and not take others' disapproval to heart.

It helps to recognize that another person's opinions are not more valid than your own and become selective about whose opinions you allow to be important to you. If you don't respect and admire someone's life, you don't want his or her opinion.

Dynamic Marriage presents an opportunity to outgrow your dependence on others' approval and acceptance. Learn to validate yourself as a person. Validation does not mean you're automatically right or things should be done your way.

If you know you're a good person and you have a right to your own perspective, then you remain open and vulnerable when your partner won't listen to you or says outrageous things.

Become conscientious parents, too: Be concerned about what your children see and hear. Your marriage is the role model for their embedded relationship scripts. When marriage is a battleground, children get lost in the melee. They recognize they are not as significant as the conflict. They learn that relationships are treacherous.

THE WAY FORWARD

When you commit to the journey toward a Dynamic Marriage, you are concentrated on what really matters. Stop over-reacting to your partner's over-reactions. It is preferable for both partners to be on the same page, but that's not your responsibility. Do it for yourself; if you can't, you are emotionally enmeshed.

If you unhook from your partner and take responsibility for your own emotional maturity, you'll feel more grounded and increase the chances that your partner may come around, but that is neither your objective nor your responsibility. That is manipulation. Your responsibility is to behave in a manner that reflects your integrity no matter what.

If you refuse to read the lines of the tired default script that leads to the battleground, if you refuse to engage in the power struggle, if you don't respond to the triggers that used to work, something is forced to change. When you are secure within yourself, there's more room to understand another's perspective. Even when the issue on the table is a "yes-no" decision, you are able to put your shared values into play and take your partner's concerns and perspectives into account.

You will notice you feel closer and warmer toward each other. Breaking the enmeshed cycle frees you to become more autonomous and more capable of true intimacy. Parenting can be the ultimate example of toxic interdependence when the primary objective of a parent is to get the validation they need from their children. You see this in the "backstage Mom" or the "soccer Dad" pushing the child to fulfill their unmet needs. This type of parenting is ALWAYS a disaster.

When parents grow up and regulate their own emotional states and sense of self, then decisions, including parenting, are founded on what best meets everyone's real needs, not egos.

THE GUIDING PRINCIPLES

The relationship principles forming the foundation of Dynamic Marriage are naïve and profound. When a couple interrupts the familiar script with new language, self-knowledge, and unexpected responses, you are forced to pause, to struggle to find new language and new ideas with which to respond, and the rhythm of the entrenched cycle is broken.

Without a predictable script, the familiar merry-go-round, the interaction becomes a free agent looking for a new framework. The space created is replaced with your conscious new "contract," where the goal is connection and trust-building, not advantage, power, and control.

In this process, you as partners are reaching toward one another, seeking to know and understand your beloved's inner world, losses and longings, thoughts, opinions, and perspectives. You become privy to and a champion of your partner's dreams and aspirations. This is a recipe for a successful partnership!

CHARTING A COURSE THROUGH CONFLICT

- Identify your default conflict/control strategies.

- Discover the roots.

- Share your discovery with your partner.

- Decide how you would like to handle conflict in the future.

- Enlist your partner's help as an accountability partner.

BLUEPRINT FOR SUCCESSFUL NEGOTIATION

- When things heat up, stop until you are back to an Open Heart position.

- Identify the actual subject matter of the current conflict.

- Is it substantive or emotional?

- Is it negotiable or forced choice?

- Articulate a desired outcome.

- Each partner should rate the importance of the topic to him or her on a scale of 1-5.

- Who is the most vested party? To whom is it most important?

- The least-vested party articulates the basis of his or her resistance and why it is important to object.

- What would be at stake if you gave in?

- Who is playing to win for the sake of winning?

EXERCISE:

This assignment will help you understand your own "back-story": the emotional history, experience, fears, and underlying beliefs that give rise to Power and Control issues in your relationship.

Generally the anger, fears, and anxieties we experience in our adult relationships arise from painful events, attitudes, and disappointments we experienced in our family of origin. When they get triggered in our marriages, it is difficult to separate the present event from the stored childhood feelings because we are over-sensitized to stored material.

Also, we tend to be attracted to people with some of the qualities of those we loved as children, and chances are these people have similar flaws and will hurt us in some of the familiar ways.

Each of you prepare the Power & Control Checklist below on your own, using the following steps:

1. Being honest but not over-thinking it, circle the feelings and behaviors that apply to you.

2. Go back over the items you have circled and write a description of a memory when you experienced the feeling or behavior.

3. Trace the feeling or behavior's history and try to link it to its roots in your childhood history.

Discussion:

When each of you have completed the checklist, create a quiet time to share with your partner what you have written. Share in the following way to stay on track and don't interrupt one another.

1. How your wounds contribute to the ways you defend and/or close yourself off.

2. The feelings and behaviors you want to change.

3. The first steps you plan to take to make the change.

4. Specifically, how your partner can support you in this.

POWER & CONTROL CHECKLIST

This checklist is designed to help you identify your default power and control strategies and the internal drivers—fears and beliefs—that trigger power and control behaviors. Work with it individually, highlighting the items that apply to you. Your discussion about the resulting insights will help you in drafting a relevant agreement. When you eliminate power and control from your relationship, you will reduce conflict and open the door to collaboration and effective communication.

External Evidence or Patterns

- Power

- Control

- Winning/Losing

- Domination

- Intimidation

- Contempt

- Dismissal

- Rage

- Withdrawal

Internal Drivers

- Anxiety/Fear

- Abandonment

- Insecurity

- Inadequacy

- Ignorance

- Incompetence

- Humiliation

- Loss of Respect

- Wounds

Beliefs & Behaviors

Scarcity

> Not enough to go around.

> Love is a limited resource.

> This is not a nurturing place.

> There is no real comfort anywhere.

Myths & Illusions

Internalized relationship scripts.

FOO modeling from parents' marriage.

Maladaptive Strategies—(Closed Heart)

Self-deception

> case-building

> blame

> denial

> deceit

Manipulation

helplessness

neediness

withdrawal

fragility

vulnerability

physical complaints

Maintaining advantage at all costs

Unregulated emotions

anger

rage

pouting

OUR AGREEMENT ON PARTNERSHIP & COLLABORATION

SECRET #4

HARMONY & ACCORD: CONFLICT VS. COMMUNICATION

The hope of a loving relationship or family is to maintain an atmosphere of harmony and accord. As you learned in the last chapter, the conduct in a relationship that interferes with productive communication and causes more conflict than any other is the struggle for power and control.

Power and control issues complicate and escalate the level of conflict in any dispute, no matter what subject is under discussion. If you as a couple are engaged in an unresolved power struggle, it is the overriding relationship problem that makes it virtually impossible to address any issue with clarity or objectivity.

When you clash over issues that surface again and again, they seem insoluble. Recurrent disputes grow until it is all you can see on the screen of your relationship. Whether the "issues" are real difficulties you face, behaviors causing conflict, values you cannot agree upon, or how you communicate about your problems—you feel stuck. The emotional climate is in a

downward spiral; disappointment, distrust, fear, anger, disillusionment, despair, and finally, hopelessness.

We explored the roots of power struggles in Secret #3. In this
chapter, we will zero in on how power and control and other
significant factors interfere with harmony and accord,[1] which
depend on good communication. Any intervention enabling
you to understand the history, beliefs, and behaviors that
are ineffective, while providing an alternative, interrupts the
conflict cycle.

You can repair broken or destructive communication patterns—anywhere along the downward slide. Mastering new
communication skills and undertaking incomplete developmental tasks renews energy and restores hope that things can
improve.

FACTORS THAT UNDERMINE COMMUNICATION

First, we'll list the significant factors that interfere with effective communication. Then we'll delve into where they come
from, how they cluster and operate, and what it takes to turn
things around.

From the beginning of your life, you were subjected to your
parents' communication patterns—that was your classroom.
Your parents were influenced by their parents. Both you
and your parents' views were further determined by gender,
ethnicity, religion, and the values and attitudes of the larger
community to which they belonged.

Children pick up on non-verbal messages as easily as spoken
words. The problem with nuances and vibes is that children

are forced to interpret the meaning from their limited perspective and dependency. A child's interpretation tends to be uncannily on target when adults are attempting to keep something from them and off-base when they really need to be accurately informed. Another confounding issue is that children pool their ignorance and pass it on as fact to younger siblings and other children.

LIST OF COMMON COMMUNICATION ROADBLOCKS

1. Power and control struggles.

2. Societal communication patterns (business as usual).

3. Family of Origin modeling.

4. Assumptions and expectations.

5. Unfinished developmental tasks.

6. Unmet and/or unacknowledged dependency needs.

7. Ego/pride.

8. Fear/denial.

The effects of power and control were discussed in depth in Secret #3. The additional roadblocks listed above contribute to a kaleidescope of factors that determine your dominant communication style, attitudes, and errors. Most of the time, you are able to maintain the communication style you adopted consciously. You learned to adapt it to meet acceptable standards of behavior in whatever environment you might find yourself.

Under sufficient stress, however, we all revert to the embedded patterns we observed early on. From the beginning of life, you absorbed prevailing biases, strategies, patterns, and attitudes of your parents and primary caretakers. Whether you accept or reject them now, they are the embedded scripts and must be uncovered to be stripped of their influence.

2. Societal Communication Patterns (Business as Usual)

In typical communication, no matter what the issue or intent, the underlying objective is to gain and maintain advantage. Analyze most conversations and you will discover the unspoken agenda is power and control, regardless of the apparent goal. The unconscious effect is that communication with an undisclosed agenda feels manipulative; undermining trust and credibility.

Conventional wisdom operates under the principle that it is not safe or wise to take anyone's words at face value, even in an intimate relationship. It is assumed, consciously or unconsciously, that there are always unstated expectations, hidden meanings, and self-serving agendas. You begin understanding how such insidious, unexamined beliefs undermine all you are trying to accomplish in your Dynamic Marriage.

In contrast, true intimacy endeavors to be totally transparent; it believes authentic power, self-esteem, and intimacy are achieved with honesty, openness, vulnerability, and a commitment to serve the best interests of the relationship. Placing the fourth Compass Point, you are developing the final skills for transforming conflict into communication.

3. Family of Origin Modeling

All families have a distinctive internal language. Families develop a shorthand all their own, which includes pet names, reprimands, criticism, facial expressions, approval and disapproval. Parental beliefs, communication patterns, and fears are instilled in ways too numerous to mention. You have a unique embedded communication script and your spouse speaks a completely different language. You and your relationship are at the mercy of both these entrenched scripts until you *discover* what they are and *dare* to co-author conscious guidelines for your communications. Deciding the manner in which you want to communicate is your task in writing the **Harmony & Accord** clause of your Agreement.

3. Assumptions & Expectations

These two habits alone can derail the most loving of relationships. Unstated expectations and unverified assumptions are deadly. They set up your spouse and your marriage for disappointment, and ultimately, for failure. The problem is you may not be aware you have them because they are so habitual and deeply buried. Part of your discovery assignment is identifying and examining them one by one as they surface.

Let me tell you a story about a client I'll call Nancy to illustrate how this operates in real life.

Nancy was a woman in her early forties. She had been a stay-at-home mother raising her two sons until they were in high school, and then she was employed managing the office for a local landscaping business. Her husband was a plumb-

er. Neither were college-educated or had previously been in therapy.

Nancy came to see me regarding fairly typical empty-nest concerns and mild depression. She never expressed any particular complaints about her husband or dissatisfaction with her marriage.

About six months into our sessions, she brought her husband with her. A few minutes into the hour, she stunned me and her husband by announcing that she wanted a divorce. Her husband was totally blindsided. He declared his love for her and asked why she wanted a divorce. This is the sad conversation that followed:

"You know how on Christmas and birthdays we each post our wish list on the refrigerator?" He nodded yes, perplexed.

"Well…not once in twenty-two years have I gotten a gift on my list from you."

"But…I like to surprise you."

"I know, but I wanted something from my list."

The wife had unstated *expectations* and the husband made unwarranted *assumptions*. The deadly duo! Obviously, inadequate and ineffective communication existed on both sides.

Another important point is related to the communication issue, but has a little different texture. In the story, the husband loved his wife—no doubt about that—but he expressed it in ways that made him feel like a good husband, not in a way that was responsive to her needs. This situation illustrates the significance of careful listening to your partner, with *curiosity* and *intention*, regarding how (s)he perceives love.[2]

Unless love is responsive to the beloved's needs or requests, it fails to hit the mark. Stubbornly or ignorantly persisting in expressing love in ways that make you feel good about yourself is not a shared activity—it is emotional self-gratification. It is not responsive to your partner's emotional needs no matter how loving your intentions. The Loved & Special exercise is an excellent tool for making these wants and needs visible. It's like the wish list posted on the refrigerator, except everyone wins.

4. Unfinished Developmental Tasks

The subject of healthy emotional support and approval in general comes up in almost every chapter because success in *all* areas of a relationship is dependent upon becoming a well-differentiated or self-referencing individual. The internal imperative for continued emotional growth is built into the human psyche and cannot be ignored without consequences. If there is a prayer that expresses this transformation, it's the one below.

Recite this prayer daily, and repeat it whenever you find yourself seeking approval or validation.

"Dear God,

Release me from all need for approval and acceptance from anyone but You. Amen."

This prayer illustrates differentiation as simply and succinctly as is possible. Two individuals having achieved a high degree of self-referencing will enjoy an exciting, compassionate, and intimate relationship. Simple, perhaps, but not easy. The work of individuation requires triumph over fear, ego, and dependency upon the approval of others.

There is an old classic western epic, *The Big Country*, in which Gregory Peck plays a character who is the perfect portrayal of a securely self-referenced individual. Watch it together. It will help you understand what being a self-referenced person looks like and how (s)he behaves. In common lingo, people talk about a differentiated person as someone who is "comfortable in his own skin."

5. Unmet and Unacknowledged Dependency Needs

Unmet dependency needs generate an endless quest for approval and validation. They force you to try constantly to convince and control others' opinions of you. You require those closest to you to prove their love in a never-ending series of subtle tests. It can be a more challenging undertaking for men than women. Our society demands that boys outgrow their dependency needs, or pretend to. This leads to denial and faking it, often showing up as "macho" behavior.

Exploring and overcoming denial to become authentic and "comfortable in your own skin," requires a couple to establish a safe and secure environment—for a three-year-old—within the relationship in order for each partner to identify and expose his or her early wounds and fears. Childhood messages about unworthiness, conditional love, ridicule for showing weakness, punishment for emotional displays like crying, etc., create shame in a young mind, shut down emotional development, and individuation, and contaminate healthy adult self-esteem.

6. Ego/Pride

Ego and pride are cover-ups for insecurity—as in the fable "The Emperor's New Clothes"—they fool only you and require everyone else in your life to join the deception. If those around you protect you, it is evidence they perceive you as too fragile to face the truth. Common hallmarks of ego and pride are: bragging, grandiosity, hogging the limelight, exaggerating accomplishments, trying to impress others, seeking approval, etc.…Make your own list. Seriously, do an inventory.

7. Fear

Almost everything in your life standing in the way of what you desire can be laid at Fear's feet. The variations are never-ending. Fear regarding: adequacy, worthiness, failure, lovability, competence, intelligence, attractiveness, body image, rejection, health, security, money….Once again, make your own list. Where there is unacknowledged fear, there is weakness.

Perhaps the greatest fear of all is having your faults and inadequacy exposed. The best defense is a preemptive strike. Expose them yourself. But first, you must expose them *to* yourself.

Fears are conceived in the past, but their energy comes from being projected into the future. The term for this kind of projected fear is anxiety. Anxiety is borrowing disaster from the future. Instead of an objective acknowledgment that bad things can happen, anxiety is expecting that the worst is inevitable. It is the opposite of faith in God.

"Perfect love casts out fear."[2] The love referred to is love for yourself first, based on the acceptance of an assurance you are made "in the image and likeness of God"[3]! What's not to love? When you say to those you care about, "I love you," what meaning does it have if the "I" is not something you value above all else? Your first responsibility is removing all barriers to unconditional love and acceptance of yourself. You cannot love anyone else unconditionally until you love yourself.

A NEW PARADIGM

Fortunately, it is never too late to master new communication skills and adopt a fresh style that works. When you are confident in a process that provides an effective method for dealing with problems and resolving disagreements, you stop avoiding them. Sidestepping, sweeping under the rug, power struggles and stone-walling create distance between partners and make the intimacy you crave elusive.

The process of crafting a meaningful contract requires cooperative negotiation and communication in order to identify and preserve the cherished values and traditions of your relationship. Collaboration replaces irritating, destructive feelings, behaviors and attitudes. In the Four Compass Points, you as partners engage in a significant, life-changing dialogue about your relationship priorities.

As individuals, you embark on a journey within: exploring, reflecting and refining, examining and rewriting embedded old scripts. Finally, this process leads to identifying and letting go of past "hurts, habits, and hang-ups"[4] and charting a new course to satisfying intimacy.

The rules and guidelines for intimate communication are considerably different from "business as usual." For starters, growing and enriching the *relationship* and the *people* in the relationship is the primary objective, not winning or losing. These principles build further toward making the shift from power and control to partnership and collaboration. Your fourth Compass Point is turning conflict into communication in order to achieve harmony and accord. The very words evoke an emotional climate of peace and contentment.

Reflect deeply upon each of the following concepts individually. Share your thoughts with one another. Discuss the ways in which you can integrate each one into your communication style. These elements will help you write the Harmony & Accord clause of your Agreement. If you consider carefully, most of them are basically the Golden Rule.

> Marriage must provide a *"holding environment"* or *"circle of security"* not only for children, but also to enable parents to grow.[5]

Security and caring provide a necessary environment for children to thrive. It makes sense that providing safety and security to one another will benefit your children. Recall the previous discussion on the emotional self as a three-year-old…you want to protect and preserve that. If you want spontaneity and play to be a primary component of your relationship and intimacy, you want a robust, secure, and uninhibited toddler at the helm!

By no means am I suggesting that childish behavior is the way for adults to run their lives. However, in the struggle to live up to your image of what it means to be a mature adult, the danger is in the tendency to suppress all the lovely things we adore in children. In order to keep those sweet, lovable traits alive in our partners and in our families, be alert and avoid these damaging acts in anger.

Alert: Never use, in anger or retaliation, sensitive information revealed to you by your partner at a time he or she felt safe to open up and be vulnerable with you. This is a major betrayal of trust and safety, which is difficult to recover.

Damage Control: Stop everything the moment you become aware of a safety violation—either by you or your partner. Rewind immediately to the moment before it happened. Ask your partner's forgiveness and help in re-playing the scene from an honest Open Heart place. Whatever the subject matter, the original discussion is now a distant second in importance to understanding what internal triggers threw you off-track.

Repair Strategy: For the partner, freeze! Stay in an Open Heart stance and protect your inner child. Remember the "Golden Rule"…how would you like your partner to respond if the roles were reversed? The person you love and trust is triggered and coming from a Closed Heart place. It only requires one of you to show restraint and compassion to get things back on track. When calm is restored, discuss the fear that was triggered and determine what the partner needs to move forward.

This is a good time to review the Rules and Guidelines in depth:

- *Loving means my beloved's needs, feelings, opinions and happiness are as important as my own.* This is a translation of the *"Golden Rule"* for relationships. It's pretty easy to see that if you truly lived this rule, your relationships would thrive. An important note on this point, this can easily be misinterpreted in a way that leads to co-dependency…*"as important AS my own"* is key. A good example of this wisdom is the safety instruction on boarding a flight: "If you are traveling with a small child, put the oxygen mask on yourself first and then on your child."

- *Nobody wins unless everybody wins, and never at the expense of another…including yourself.* Once again, simply another way of expressing the central message in the Golden Rule. It's hard to believe this simple, fair standard is so difficult to live. But in a world where so much is measured in competitive terms, a world of winners and losers, it is difficult to live in this generous and peaceful manner. Your best opportunity is in your marriage and family. If we model this lifestyle with our children and confront sibling rivalry where the objective is to win at the expense of another, then we have a chance to impact the future.

- *No blame or judgment of another: giving one another the benefit of the doubt.*

Not being judgmental is really about listening, respect, and responsibility. Scripture teaches: "Judge not that you be not judged." Blaming another is a way of not taking responsibility for your own actions. Giving another the benefit of the doubt takes the time to discover another's intentions rather than taking offense or making assumptions…always a dangerous thing to do. Besides, is it not what you would want someone to do for you?

- *Treat one another with the same love and respect you want to receive.*

  Does this really require an explanation? But you probably need to be reminded again, especially when stress and conflict are in the relationship.

- *Listen with **curiosity** and with **intention** to **appreciate** and **understand**.*

  Isn't this the way you want to be listened to? But the words in this concept are much more profound and powerful than you might realize at first glance. You and your beloved are well-advised to have a serious discussion about the importance of developing these particular listening skills. *Curiosity* and *intention* to *appreciate* another's perspective and *understand* that person's feelings is a rare gift. Mastering these two concepts alone will transform the way you communicate in every area of life. In the business world, these gifts are considered hallmarks of effective leaders.

Alert: When you find yourself contradicting or convincing one another, you are violating the above.

- *Seek first to understand and second to be understood.*

  A primary maxim in all sales training is: "People don't care what you know, until they know you care." Remember the fair and honest discussion in Secret #2? This maxim is an expansion of the previous item. *Curiosity and intention to appreciate and understand* first is the way you earn the right to be heard.

- *Honesty involves telling your truth in **this** moment, relevant to **this** discussion, not a hidden past.*

  Bringing up past hurts and offenses in a discussion is a diversion tactic or power play when you feel you are losing the argument. Make it a rule to stick to the subject at hand, being fair and honest. If unresolved issues and hurts interfere with moving forward, they need to be addressed in an intentional way—to forgive and put them behind you once and for all. Continually sabotaging a present discussion by repeatedly expressing anger and/or hurt over past offenses is not honest, fair, or respectful. We will discuss resolving thorny issues at the end of this chapter.

- *Ego is defensive: the enemy of love and real intimacy by its selfishness and closed heart stance.*

  John Gottman[7] cites defensiveness as one of four destructive relationship behaviors that lead to divorce. Defensiveness is a product of ego and ego is evidence of immaturity.

  As discussed previously, it is often based on a belief that you have to be perfect to be loved. We have referred to the developmental tasks of adulthood with the goal of becoming differentiated or self-referencing. An unbridled ego is a signal that you are still dependent on others' approval in order to feel good about yourself. One way it shows up is defensiveness: taking things personally and finding fault with others. All of these tactics undermine intimate and authentic relationships.

- *When you are sure you are right or need to be—you are probably wrong (EGO is driving you).*

  One behavior that is a sure sign of ego steering the boat is certainty about being right...or the need to be right. Ask yourself why: Why is it important to be right? What is at stake if you are not right? What is the consequence of being wrong? The answers to these questions is in your history. Again, a need to be right rises out of conditional love and a belief that you have to be perfect to be loved. The internal scripts need to be scrutinized and updated. Recognize the stakes now are not the same as for the helpless, dependent child.

  Look for opportunities to admit you are wrong. It's fun practice! Try saying, "I owe you an apology." Or, "I'm sorry," "It was my fault," or "My mistake." Humility is a courageous and admirable trait. It feels good and the rewards are immense. Your spouse, children, and colleagues will be stunned!

- *Every challenge offers myriad possibilities; the real problem is in limiting beliefs, feelings, attitudes.*

Curiosity is a wonderful trait to nurture. Normally nothing new occurs until the old way stops working. Get ahead of the curve, explore new ways as a practice. Rather than reading catastrophe into every roadblock, become curious, shift perspective, look for the learning, welcome the growth, unlock hidden potential.

• *A slight shift in perspective—understanding from another's point of view can create miracles.*

You may have watched "Judge Judy" or some other legal show. One person tells their story and you are totally sold on their side. Then the opposing party tells their side and your find yourself shifting to uncertainty and then weighing the two sets of "facts" and trying to decide who is right and who is wrong. In an intimate relationship it is rarely as simple as right and wrong…black and white. But you can be sure there are two sides to every story, and both deserve to be heard and considered.

Everyone has his or her own truth. It is a mark of maturity and wisdom to become curious about the perspective of another and try to join them rather than convince them. It is difficult to sustain conflict when you become curious and willing to "walk a mile in another's shoes."

IN SUMMARY

To reduce the complications associated with power and control in a relationship, it is important to recognize and understand the inner motivations at work. Power and control are attempts to keep unacknowledged fear at bay in order to feel secure. Therefore, the objective is to establish a personally controlled environment that provides a sense of security.

Intimate relationships stir up dependency needs that were not met in childhood: loneliness, helplessness, fear, rejection, abuse, injustice....All the unexamined and unresolved stuff of childhood can be activated under duress. People attempt to control both others and circumstances to ensure that none of the painful events are repeated or painful memories triggered.

The problem with exercising power and control over people you love is that it will more likely result in causing the alienation and rejection you are desperate to avoid. Intimacy and control are mutually exclusive. Intimacy requires the willingness to be interdependent, to risk for love.

Loving requires risk. Loving requires the courage to face your fears and the strength to go wherever it takes you. Your relationship is a joint creation by you and your beloved, a partnership. Power and control do not safeguard your relationship. Instead, they divide and destroy.

IN SEARCH OF ILLUSION

Security is an illusion; in this life, there is none of any kind. No realistic way exists to protect any of the things that matter most to you: your beloved, your children, your income, your home, your future economic security. The amount of time and energy spent in the pursuit of security is time robbed from enjoying the truly good things present in your life now.

The time and energy wasted in attempting to control those you love will undermine their trust in your love. Instead of control, develop genuine curiosity about them: their interests, their anxieties, their hopes, and their dreams. Look for opportunities to share thoughts and feelings about yourself. Risk it all for the sake of all. Tackle the personal interior healing necessary to be strong enough to risk.

FRIENDS & ENEMIES

True self-esteem is the opposite of ego. Ego is an enemy that masks as a friend. Ego is a cover for low self-esteem and insecurity…a bogus mask that fools only you while everyone else eventually sees through it. When you employ this shield, it creates a defensive stance that alienates those with whom you long to be close.

Look for opportunities to admit wrongdoing, to apologize, to acknowledge a fault even before there is an issue. Monitor your tendency to blame others for what is not the way you think it should be.

Pay attention to your feelings and responses. Monitor your communication and behavior and the responses you get from others. Was it difficult or easy? Did you feel good or bad? Did it make you feel more than or less than? Did you feel that you lost or gained status in others' eyes? How did the others respond to you?

Seek occasions to practice humility. Be the first to own your shortcomings. Everyone has faults, limitations, and weaknesses. Be the rare person who has enough self-confidence and security to admit faults, to laugh at him or herself, and to take responsibility for the consequences of errors and mistakes.

Don't allow others' response to you to undermine the new behaviors you are developing. It takes courage and consistency to master new behaviors, but it's well worth the effort. Keep up the good work.

*"All my suffering is the result of my decision that something (or someone) isn't as it **should** be."*

COMMUNICATING EFFECTIVELY WITH ROADBLOCKS AND CONFLICT:

Listen to one another with *curiosity and intention to appreciate and understand.*

- Repeat what you heard before responding:
  - Receiver, "Can I tell you what I heard you say?"
  - Sender, "Can you tell me what you heard me say?"

- When you both agree on what was said, respond *on topic* from an open heart.

Continue the interaction using the above format each time the speaker changes. Communication theory has a strict rule: *the sender is responsible for the message.* If a response indicates that your intended message is misunderstood by the receiver, it is incumbent on the sender to clarify until the message is received as intended before moving on. If the sender responds to a misinterpreted message, the negotiation will go astray.

If it becomes clear to the sender that the receiver is not interested in amending the intended message, there is an unspoken power agenda at play, so there is no advantage in proceeding at this time. Here are some clues to watch for: the receiver decides to take offense; tweaks your words so they have a negative meaning not intended; interprets your response as a personal insult or attack; brings up past griev-ances; resorts to name-calling, blame, accusations, etc.

Either party has the responsibility to postpone the discussion when it becomes clear one party is in a Closed-Heart place. This is a necessary step to protect the relationship. It should be done lovingly, with understanding and patience; a Closed-Heart (hurt three-year-old) is in the grip of unacknowledged fear. Next time it may be you who is unable to engage as a self-referenced adult and needs your partner to treat you with compassion. Whenever an interaction becomes heated, postpone the discussion. Poking around in open wounds is abusive.

> *"The person who knows your wounds and sees them as faults is not a partner."* [9]

Remember the concept of the relationship as a third enti-ty—a partnership in which each partner invests. Normally when people invest, they willingly give up something of value in order to invest in something that promises a greater return on their investment. Isn't this a good model for how a mar-riage should operate? Sometimes it means giving up some-thing of perceived value, such as ego or power—for a greater return, such as intimacy and a dynamic working relationship.

MY GOALS FOR HARMONY & ACCORD

EXERCISES

Discover your partner's needs, desires, and preferences, as a playful joint adventure, like a game of *Clue*. Ask outright questions like:

"Is that an expectation?"

"Are you making an assumption?"

"What are your expectations for this evening, weekend, vacation, activity, event?"

"I assume that means…?"

1. Identify as many **Expectations and Assumptions** in your relationship as you can think of.

2. Celebrate those you agree on.

3. Explore those you don't agree on.

4. Decide which ones you want to keep and which you choose to discard or update.

Make a pact to voice expectations and check out assumptions moving forward. Agree on cue words you can use to help each other succeed in your communication goals.

Discussion:

Before drafting the Conflict & Communication clause in your Relationship Agreement, review the Checklist & Discussion at the end of Secret #3. Engage in an honest conversation about the ways Power and Control can disrupt effective communication.

When conflict arises: Who generally prevails? Who gives in? Why? How long does it last?

Do I think of myself as aggressive or passive? Do I provoke fear or use intimidation as a tool to get my way?

What is the intimate information I have about my spouse that gives me the power to use fear and intimidation?

Where is my spouse most vulnerable? Because?

Identify the primary strategies each of you employs to get what you want.

How do you go about creating emotional distance when you need it?

Be mindful that control can be passive as well as aggressive: withdrawal, resistance, stonewalling, door-knobbing, helplessness, manipulation, pouting, withholding affection, the silent treatment, etc. are all passive ways of exerting control and power.

Do some soul-searching and consider these questions:

1. What makes me feel the need for control?

2. What fears motivate it?

3. How do I go about it?

4. How does my spouse control?

5. In what areas does control show up?

6. How does my spouse's control affect me?

7. How does it make me feel?

OUR AGREEMENT ON HARMONY & ACCORD

PART TWO

BODY, MIND & SPIRIT

Part II: Body, Mind & Spirit

PROLOGUE

In Part I: The Four Compass Points, you constructed a foundation of important concepts and skills for you as a couple to undergird your agreement. You focused on your shared connection, your values, your partnership, and your communication. Now that you have those critical Four Compass Points in place, you will begin to negotiate each area of your agreement—clause by clause—using the insights you have into your own inner world and the practical tools you have learned.

As you venture into each specific area in the following chapters, the agreements you made in the Four Compass Points will be your guidance system in all the agreements that follow. Consider all Four Compass Points as forming the GPS for every area moving forward.

Work your way through each of the remaining chapters, you will find areas where you are in general agreement that you will breeze right through. Congratulate yourselves. Celebrate the things you do well together. Other chapters may challenge you and your marriage to the core. Things you have avoided talking about in the past can and will be faced. No marriage will have problems in all areas; nor will any relationship be trouble-free in every area. So you have an opportunity for the "do-overs" you've always wanted, if you dare. Do you?

In proceeding through *Discovering a Dynamic Marriage*, remember this voyage is one of discovery. Discovering is not a passive concept; it requires action and daring. Whether or not you believe you need help in a particular area, read all the chapters, and do the exercises together. Now is the right time and this is the right place to confront things that simmer beneath the surface, stealing intimacy and vitality from your relationship. You will discover something in the exploration that will enrich you and your relationship. Adhering to the rules and guidelines creates a safe, structured process for working your way through to a mutual agreement that supports your health and well-being.

At times in the course of the Dynamic Marriage journey, you may find things to celebrate and feel good about. You may encounter difficulties that other marriages in your circle are struggling with. You may learn something that will enable you to understand those couples' pain and maybe help them resolve it. Perhaps you will give them a copy of *Discovering a Dynamic Marriage* or refer them to the website.

IN SEARCH OF RELEVANCE

Discovering a Dynamic Marriage is designed to support relationships at any age or stage of life. You may be reading this book in anticipation of being married, or you may be recently married, becoming parents, blending families in a second marriage, raising a family, or empty-nesting and retiring. Because this book seeks to be relevant to marriages at all ages and stages, the following sections include important information for couples with children and families. Don't sidestep these sections by thinking they are irrelevant to you because you don't have kids.

As you learned in Part I, your embedded scripts from early childhood continue to impact who you are in a relationship. Working your way through each section will continue to increase your understanding of yourself and what you learned growing up. If your children are grown, you may recognize mistakes you made in raising your children. Humbly sharing these new insights with them can help them better understand themselves and perhaps avoid repeating the same mistakes with their children.

You may see that flawed parenting practices your children learned from you are being employed with your grandchildren. When you get to Secret #11, you will discover it is generally not wise to tell your kids how to parent. But handing them a copy of this book with a statement along the lines of, "I wish I had read this book when I was raising you; I would have been a better parent," will generally be well-received and may open much-needed lines of communication.

PART II: BODY, MIND & SPIRIT

Part II concentrates on body, mind, and spirit. As you should be aware by now, everything starts with the self—even intimacy.

Secret #5 concentrates on the physical and health aspects of you, your partner, and children. The health chapter looks into every factor affecting the family's health: addictions, eating habits, nutrition, illness, and fitness. Concerns about obesity, self-destructive behaviors, excesses, or compulsions show up in this area. Differences regarding children's nutritional needs can be a point of contention. A family member with a chronic illness is difficult for any family. Health can be a challenging area for some couples.

Secret #6 focuses on the mental and emotional health of all the family members. Everything you did in Part I was in the service of your mental and emotional health. In this chapter, you will further explore the issues that stand in the way of what you want, either in yourself or your relationship. It is a commitment to lifelong learning and development. In writing your agreement, you will want to articulate your commitment to support the mental and emotional health of one another and negotiate how you will handle potentially sensitive matters.

Secret #7 explores the spiritual and religious underpinnings of your relationship. It is already established that a shared faith is a great basis for a relationship, but according to the statistics, it offers no guarantee for success. Approach this chapter from the viewpoint of exploring the beliefs each of you hold about life, love, and God, our purpose for being on this earth, and the promise of a hereafter. Many couples have never shared their innermost thoughts on this subject, and it can bring you closer together.

On the other side of the coin, if you have differing beliefs, keep your heart open, and be curious, appreciative, and respectful. Be alert for clues to a dimension in your beloved that is new to you and acknowledge it.

OUR GOALS FOR PART II: BODY, MIND & SPIRIT

SECRET #5

HEALTH & FITNESS

Health and fitness may not sound like high-conflict subjects. Hopefully, they aren't in your marriage. But in some relationships, they are loaded areas. When you consider dietary habits, nutrition, eating disorders, obesity, chronic illness, allergies, congenital conditions, dietary restrictions, substance abuse, addictions, and compulsive fitness practices, you can see how complicated this area of life can be.

The health and fitness values and practices of you and your partner can enhance or interfere with a harmonious and mutually supportive relationship. When couples have similar beliefs on the subject and agree about how these values and practices should show up in their lives, it can enrich and deepen the bond.

As in most areas, there are healthy and unhealthy ways of relating to it. The perception that your partner is invested in your health, fitness, or appearance for his or her own sake rather than yours—no matter what the rationale—can be a source of conflict. Where this is the case, it is either a power/

control issue or indicative of fusion: my beloved is an extension of me and/or my partner's appearance and behavior reflects on me.

If either your spouse or you have a history of parental or peer expectations and pressure regarding health, weight, body image, appearance, etc., it can be a very delicate area. This history—as well as a history of illness, body image issues, overweight or eating disorders—needs to be disclosed, discussed, and dealt with together. Overemphasis on body image or a parent's unhealthy or inappropriate interest in appearance, weight, or fitness can have a lingering influence into adulthood and make a person defensive or resistant to any reference to the subject.

If core differences exist in the history or preferences between partners or an active addiction or OCD exists, it will be difficult to do the work of writing the Health & Fitness section of the Dynamic Marriage agreement until these issues are addressed. This chapter will be divided into sections so you can consider them in depth, one at a time. Some subjects may show up under more than one of the broad headings below. For instance, a given practice may not reach a level that merits a definition of addiction or compulsion, but if it causes conflict in your relationship, it has to be negotiated.

- Addictions and compulsions

- Adult eating patterns

- Establishing healthy eating habits

- Congenital, chronic, or life-threatening conditions

- Fitness regimens

ADDICTIONS & COMPULSIONS

What constitutes an addiction? By definition, addiction refers to a practice or habit you are no longer able to control. Addictions are not always easy to identify. The addicted person is usually in denial and unable to identify or admit when the behavior has crossed the line. Too often, those closest to the person are co-conspirators in the self-deception game. In the substance abuse world, this co-conspiracy is called "enabling."

The closest people, generally the spouse and family, collude in keeping the problem hidden or even in keeping the victim supplied. A multitude of reasons exist for enabling. In the first place, addictions tend gradually to creep up on you and on the family. Secondly, disclosure sets in motion a wave of aftershocks that are difficult to predict and prepare for. Unacknowledged addiction in a family is called "the elephant in the room" for good reason.

Confronting an unacknowledged addiction requires courage and adequate preparation. It is a difficult and challenging situation that will likely cause resistance in the abuser and total disruption for everyone in the system. Seek professional help if you are considering an intervention in an addiction. When an abuser is ready to deal with the addiction, it should be with the support of an established recovery program with a history of success, such as a Twelve-Step program (Alcoholics Anonymous) or Celebrate Recovery.

When the subject of addiction is mentioned, most people immediately think of substance abuse: alcohol, tobacco, street drugs, or prescription drugs. Addictive substances chemically alter the brain's emotional centers and provide escape from anxiety, vulnerability, and pain. Behavioral types of addiction are subtle and more difficult to recognize and/or diagnose. It is so important to understand this material, in order to clear the field for your Dynamic Marriage, that we need to take a look at each of these areas separately in the following sections.

WHAT IS AN EATING DISORDER?

Eating disorders are classified as anxiety disorders that share many characteristics of addictions and compulsions:

- **Anorexia:** resistance to maintaining a healthy weight, obsessive fear of weight gain, unrealistic perception of body image. Popularly thought to be confined to adolescent girls, anorexia is increasingly seen in boys and middle-aged women. Being underweight can interrupt menstruation, cause bone loss, reduce skin integrity, and increase risk of heart attacks and related heart disease. Untreated, a point is reached where the damage becomes irreversible and results in death.

- **Bulimia:** cyclical binge eating followed by purging or fasting. Purging consists of forced vomiting, laxatives/diuretics, and/or compulsive exercise. Purging sensitizes normal functioning and the urge to vomit may persist even when bulimia is overcome and eventually destroys tooth enamel.

- **Bingeing:** "compulsive overeating," binge eating without purging. This disorder is more common than bulimia or anorexia, develops in a broad range of ages, and is not limited to specific populations.

- **Compulsive Overeating:** differs from binge eating disorder in that it is not cyclical but a lifestyle. People who eat more than needed suffer from an increase in emotional and physical stress and may become obese.

Although eating disorders fall under a diagnosis of anxiety disorders, certain foods cause chemical changes in the brain, especially in the case of sugar. Sugar causes a chemical reaction in the brain which metabolizes similarly to alcohol—the source of the term "sugar high."[1] Children and adults with autism and ADHD seem to be ultra-sensitive to sweets addiction and the effects of a high sugar snack can cause immediate noticeable changes in behavior in a child. Adults learn to moderate the observable behavioral effects, but the "high" still occurs.

Most addictions are, at their core, a means to escape and feel temporary relief from pain, loss, and longing. The sense of power and control that comes from addictive substances and/or behaviors can be seductive, thus perpetuating the behavior.

a. A History of Eating Disorders

Eating disorders finally came to public attention as a widespread problem in the 1980s and were thought to be an adolescent disorder. Over the past thirty years, the onset of puberty has moved toward an increasingly younger age and is now common in preadolescent girls. Under current standards of beauty, adolescent girls feel they have to be underweight to measure up. Professional models range in age from 13-17, are much taller than the average, and underweight to an extent that undermines health. Those images are the ideals young girls starve to grow into. The resulting lifetime of physical and emotional consequences remain largely unconsidered by the youngster.

When we see photographs of female movie idols from half-a-century ago who were considered the epitome of sex appeal—Marilyn Monroe, Rita Hayworth, Jane Russell, Jayne Mansfield—they were all voluptuous, with womanly curves, and they were celebrated for it. Fortunately, there is a growing movement to reverse the trend of idealizing thinness. Meryl Streep, Catherine Zeta-Jones, Kate Winslet, and Debra Messing are prime examples of notable celebrities who have the self-esteem and courage to maintain a healthy weight and body-image.

A few stars have publically denounced the practice of airbrushing cover photos to make them look thinner than they are. *Vogue* magazine recently adopted a policy of using only average-weight models over age sixteen. Other prominent companies that make cosmetics and beauty products are mounting ad campaigns targeting this issue.

Within a family, the early signs of eating disorders are generally elusive and easy to overlook. As is the case with most addictive disorders, eating disorders begin with innocuous or even beneficial behavior shifts. For example, a chubby youngster succumbs to peer or parental pressure and decides to lose a few pounds and feels good about it.

The ability to overcome hunger makes the child feel powerful and in control. The feeling of power and control becomes linked to hunger and gradually develops into an objective itself. Food intake is gradually reduced, high calorie food eliminated, portion sizes become miniscule, and family meals are avoided. Eating alone and gradual social isolation are common signals.

As awareness has grown and the appearance-conscious Baby Boomer generation has aged, eating disorders have begun to show up increasingly in middle-aged women. Aging celebrities in the spotlight struggled to slim down to and maintain their lowest lifetime weight. An underweight teenage body becomes associated with youthful beauty, exuberance, and self-esteem.

When the main source of a young person's identity is in personal appearance—external rather than internal—beauty is no longer an adjective but an objective. In time, the pursuit of whatever youthful age has been adopted as the victim's internalized standard for beauty becomes an obsession. Spouses and parents feel helpless in dealing with the condition.

b. Obsessive Compulsive Disorder & Exercise

A related obsessive compulsive disorder—popularly known as OCD—often goes hand-in-hand with eating disorders when the obsession is associated with appearance. Compulsive exercise and ritualized eating and fitness regimens, which cause outrage when interfered with, are evidence of a possible OCD condition. Eating disorders and compulsive exercise are often found together, but either can exist without the other. The question of a concerned observer may be, "Where do you draw the line?"

Signs to look for:

- Eating or fitness takes on a ritual aspect.

- Events have to occur, or foods have to be consumed, in a certain order or pattern.

- The ritual grows as new steps are added.

- The individual becomes unduly upset when there is interference or interruption.

- Life begins to be organized around the compulsion.

- Attempts are made to conceal the compulsive behaviors from the family.

If you suspect a family member is showing any of the signs listed above and is resistant to talking about it, it is wisest to drop it for now. A person in the grip of addiction or OCD is not able to be rational or objective. Don't get into a conflict; it will prevent further progress on your Dynamic Marriage Agreement. Attacking or preventing the behavior does not address the underlying cause.

These conditions are difficult to diagnose and treat because the symptoms spring from a deep-seated anxiety. Talk with a professional specializing in the area of concern so you can determine exactly what you are dealing with and how you should proceed.

c. Body Dysmorphia

In the above conditions, one of the complications is a condition known technically as "body dysmorphic disorder" (BDD). It is a psychological disorder characterized by excessive preoccupation with imagined defects in physical appearance. BDD is classified as an anxiety disorder and is a variation of obsessive-compulsive disorder. This manifests as a distorted view of the individual's own body image. You might look and see a person who is too thin, but the sufferer looks in the mirror and sees a chubby person.

A distortion exists between the image seen by the eyes and how it is interpreted by the brain. No amount of reassurance or positive feedback will change the perception. This condition requires professional treatment.

BDD sometimes occurs in a person who experiences sudden extreme weight loss or radical alterations in appearance as a result of a surgical procedure. In these cases, it may be temporary if it is not due to OCD. Compassionate support in updating old tapes and integrating the new information is essential.

ADULT EATING PATTERNS

Differences between partners regarding eating habits can be a constant source of conflict. Food is deeply embedded in the psyche at an early age and is inextricably linked with love, comfort, and survival. There is a reason the favorite foods of childhood linger through adulthood as "comfort foods." What comes to mind immediately when you read those words? Certain foods or meals come to mind, and if you allow yourself to linger on it for a moment, feelings will come up as well. It's all interconnected to our earliest experiences.

The food choices of the family you grew up in (FOO) constitute your defaults and cravings. Meat and potatoes, casseroles, ethnic foods, fried foods, pasta, soups, sandwiches and salads, high carbohydrate foods, sweets and desserts, junk food and fast food—whatever you grew up with will linger as a subconscious attraction. Think about what you want to eat when you have had a bad day and want to comfort yourself.

Some other complicating health issues include adult obesity, which always has health implications, and is a source of concern for the partner. A spouse may require daily accommodation if he or she is vegetarian or vegan, has an allergy requiring a special diet, or has a health condition or illness with strict dietary restrictions.

Before Charles and Yvette were married, they were fully aware Yvette was a strict vegetarian and Charles was a meat and potatoes guy. Charles even went on the annual hunting trip with the men in his family. From the beginning, Yvette established that she would not prepare or eat meat. Charles was introduced to vegetarian foods for the first time.

Charles was sensitive to Yvette's dietary restrictions in selecting foods, especially in restaurants, often asking questions about the ingredients in dishes. Charles' family celebrated holidays with traditional meals. Even though Yvette made no demands, accommodating a vegetarian impacted the traditions. Charles' mom wanted to make appropriate dishes so Yvette had more choices. Yvette often avoided even common foods like mashed potatoes and dressings because they might contain animal products. Sometimes, she inquired about the ingredients before eating the dish.

Differing dietary needs complicate everyday choices. One meal or two meals? Does one person yield because it is easier and saves time? How do you handle holiday meals if the family features meat as the central part of the meal? What happens when Charles and Yvette host the holiday meal for his family? What about restaurants? Does one partner give up a favorite restaurant because it doesn't accommodate the dietary needs of a spouse?

Projecting into the future, how will the children be raised? How will dietary differences be discussed without one spouse influencing the child's choices? How do you entertain friends who are not vegetarians?

Food becomes a potential battleground for a new relationship…or not. Yvette and Charles came to terms with their differences and continue to evolve as situations arise. Charles has learned to enjoy vegetarian dishes. Yvette is no longer as rigid and has stopped asking questions about hidden ingredients of meals served by family and friends.

Their joint commitment to put the relationship first has resulted in unexpected acts of love and respect. On Father's Day, Yvette surprised Charles with his favorite pulled pork dinner. She did not eat the meat, but even preparing a meat dish was an act of love outside her comfort zone. Charles voluntarily stopped hunting. He joins his family on the annual trip for fellowship with the guys, but no longer hunts game himself.

ESTABLISHING HEALTHY EATING HABITS

Decide together what nutritional values you want to put into practice as a couple and in your family. Being consistent is crucial. The latest research continues to validate that "You are what you eat." Good health depends on good nutrition and regular exercise. The exercises and discussion questions at the end of this chapter will help you to identify what you need to write your Health & Fitness Agreement.

Sabotage is an elusive, always available, frustrating weapon. A spouse who continually brings banned foods into the house contrary to agreed-upon nutritional values or takes kids out for fast food, sabotages the agreement. Here is the Franklin family's story, illustrating sabotage in the parents' health decisions.

> Peter is the oldest child in the Franklin family. He was diagnosed with autism at the age of three. Both parents agreed to follow the best treatment advice of the experts on the subject. Peter's mother was opposed to medications, so she continued to research alternative and natural autism treatment protocols.
>
> One evening, Peter's grandmother brought over homemade brownies for dessert. The children were playing quietly after dinner while mother cleaned the kitchen before dessert. Within ten minutes of eating the brownie, Peter turned into a whirling dervish. He was twirling around the room, talking wildly, and couldn't settle down. All the adults were aware of the change and the cause. It was clear Peter was ultra-sensitive to sugar.

Peter's dad was a recovering alcoholic who had addressed his addiction at age twenty and maintained sobriety for many years. But, he continued to be a sugar addict and bring high-sugar foods into the house. Mom's research discovered a diet specifically shown to be helpful in autistic and ADHD children.

She enlisted her husband's commitment to changing the family's nutrition for Peter's sake. The diet eliminated dairy, gluten, and sugar. The parents explained the new nutrition plan to the children in a way they understood and accepted. Mom cleared the house of all forbidden foods and restocked with foods allowed on the nutrition plan.

Dad continued to indulge in high-sugar treats off-site. In time, the kids caught on to Dad's inconsistency and felt deceived. Dad's trunk was stocked with candy bars and sodas and discarded candy wrappers littered his car. Gradually, the forbidden foods began to creep back into the house; Dad would bring home pizza for dinner and ice cream for dessert. Favorite cereals high in gluten and sugar, frozen waffles, and Pop Tarts showed up in the pantry. Dad poured copious amounts of catsup (high sugar content) on everything on the kids' plates.

It was a losing situation for Mom; Dad played the hero and cast Mom as the warden. It was a battle she could not win without her husband's support, so finally, she gave up. Sabotage is deadly in a marriage.

In this case, the Franklin family's dad was the one who manipulated with food, but the children learned manipulation too. Children learn to manipulate with food at an early age.

A child refuses to eat certain foods. Later, he overhears the parents saying, "Johnny won't eat peas", and confirms that the child won and makes him feel powerful. The child's position determines what foods they purchase and serve.

Children won't give up the advantage once they gain it. Mom becomes a short order cook preparing separate meals for each child. Children bargain for forbidden foods, like candy and sweet treats, in return for tasks or behaviors the parents want them to do. It's a trap that parents fall into all too easily if they don't have an agreement to back each other up.

When one parent is too preoccupied or harried to stay focused on being consistent, children will take advantage. They learn that manipulation and deviousness are effective tactics for getting their way, without consideration of the cost to others. That's when the partner needs to step in and call the game.

It's not good partnering or good parenting to send children out into the world being manipulative. They conclude the rules don't apply to them and they scheme to get around them. Manipulation is a form of dishonesty and others see them as devious. Parents have to be diligent and make it a family value to be honest, cooperative and considerate of others. Good parenting is not a job for wimps!

CONGENITAL, CHRONIC, OR LIFE-THREATENING ILLNESSES

A family member with a congenital or chronic condition is a drain on family resources physically, emotionally, and financially. A medical condition impacts holidays and vacations as well as everyday activities. A critical health crisis or life-threatening illness destabilizes the entire system. Even if the healthy children are old enough to understand the afflicted member's needs and the parents' unavailability, the children still suffer deprivation and feel resentment, which results in guilt and shame.

Round-the-clock care of an elderly, chronically, or congenitally ill person usually defaults to one family member. The others flee to avoid the responsibility and discomfort. The caretaker assumes an additional full-time job that negatively impacts the couple's relationship. The caretaker takes on the role, generally at the expectation of the system, without awareness or consideration of the toll it will take on him or her. This situation results in the primary caregiver having no time for him or herself, and the person even risks being censured when a request is made for temporary respite.

Accidents and sudden severe illnesses are generally crisis situations that create a time warp in family life and may have long-term effects on the healthy children's mental health and emotional adjustment. When a family has to face this situation, it is crucial to seek support from a professional therapist specializing in children. All the family members need help in processing their conflicting feelings.

The same goes for the parents. Couples with an ill or disabled child or who are suffering the death of a child have a very high divorce rate. They need a competent therapist with a specialty in supporting parents through grief or difficult circumstances. The last thing the healthy or surviving children need is to deal with a divorce on top of their other losses.

FITNESS REGIMENS

Exercise and fitness are essential to health—within reason. Other than the OCD fitness issues we already discussed above, fitness activities that dominate weekends or evenings and interfere with shared parenting responsibilities during the times free of work and school can cause conflict between partners. Bike racing, golfing, marathons, competitive sports, and weightlifting are time-consuming activities that may not lend themselves to the active child-rearing years of marriage. This area is one where the fairness rule must be invoked. It is important to schedule equal time for each parent to pursue a reasonable fitness activity.

Finding exercise opportunities you enjoy together is a good alternative. Engage in family sports like bicycling, volleyball, softball, roller-blading, skiing, hiking, dancing, and martial arts. Many activities exist that can be shared by a couple or a family. The local YMCA is just one of many places to spend a few weekend hours working out, swimming, or playing paddle ball or volleyball together. Most YMCA facilities offer child care for infants and toddlers while the older children and parents play.

The most important thing is that each family member feels valued and gets his or her fair share of the family resources: time, energy, and money. Making such time a priority will pay off later when the children are teenagers and still want to spend time with the family when most kids their age would prefer to be with friends.

EXERCISES

1. Plan B: What if a health crisis were to impact our family? How would we handle it?

2. What are your comfort foods? Make a list of them.

3. How do you use your comfort foods now?

4. What triggers the need or craving for them?

5. How often does this craving occur?

6. Does it undermine your overall health and fitness goals?

Discussion:

1. Think about and share the history of how your comfort foods became comfort foods.

2. Share the history of parental messages and expectations about weight, appearance, and body image.

3. Do these messages haunt you now?

4. Do you have concerns about the messages you may be conveying to your children?

5. How can you support one another's fitness goals? Be specific.

6. Do you have a health and fitness strategy for yourselves and your family?

7. What decisions do you need to make in order to include personal and family health goals in your agreement?

OUR AGREEMENT ON HEALTH & FITNESS

Secret #6

INTELLECTUAL & EMOTIONAL: INDIVIDUAL & COUPLE

In Part I, you learned about the concept of marriage as the "crucible," the relationship where you carry on the internal imperative to grow, differentiate, develop intimacy skills, and become a mature self-referencing person. In this chapter, you will continue to focus on the journey into yourself and your impact on the world.

The voyage within includes personal growth, intellectual development, and emotional well-being. Increasing your impact on the world outside might include continuing or completing formal education, professional development, career advancing certifications, and/or pursuing graduate degrees.

At the end of Secret #6, your beloved and you will share the plans and dreams you have for yourself in both important areas. Too often, in the hustle and bustle of family life, couples neglect to keep each other up-to-date on the shifts in their internal world—their dreams, hopes, plans, perhaps even career changes. This situation is particularly true if you anticipate that voicing those changes might meet with resistance from your partner or upset the household's equilibrium.

Intellectual and emotional growth are very personal, at the core of your individual being. Taking the risk—daring—to reveal who you are becoming, giving your partner the space to respond without pulling you off-course, is at the very center of differentiation and intimacy. The discussion between you and your partner that leads to an agreement in this area is of critical significance to individual development and the richness of your relationship.

INTELLECTUAL DEVELOPMENT

In the past decade, a great deal of research has been conducted into the way the brain develops prior to birth, in early childhood, adolescence, and as adults. It used to be thought that events occurring before memory had no effect.[1] It was also believed the brain was largely developed by the ages of six to eight, primarily concentrated in the years even before beginning elementary school. When that was the prevailing wisdom, parents tended to disregard traumas in infancy and toddler years. Now we know that early childhood—and even pre-birth—trauma shows up in adulthood as a variety of mental health diagnoses, dysfunctions and addictions.[2]

These beliefs led parents to largely relinquish to schools the job of educating children. Recent research, however, advocates that intentional efforts to promote intellectual growth, emotional well-being, and self-awareness should be a substantial objective of parenting from the moment of conception and throughout the preschool years.

Recent research in brain development indicates that the emotional state of the mother during pregnancy has longterm consequences on mental and emotional health of the child and the roots of issues are often difficult to trace.

Many changes in the last half of the twentieth century changed the face of the American family. The educational level of the population—particularly among women—rose and gave rise to today's burgeoning number of wives and mothers earning college degrees and having careers of their own. This trend included fathers becoming increasingly active in parenting and family life. The divorce rate rose rapidly throughout these decades and has stabilized at 50 percent for the past half century. As a result, single parent families comprise a large segment of the population. Everything about the traditional American family has become anything but traditional.

WHAT THE EXPERTS SAY

The evidence of "brain plasticity" around the turn of the 21st century informed the entire field of physical, mental, and emotional health. We have long been aware that stress is detrimental to health. Now we understand why. Stress inhibits the intellectual and emotional development of children and undermines physical, emotional, and mental health in adults.[3] With the benefit of this knowledge, support of emotional well-being into your partnership agreement is an essential element.

It has been proposed by leaders in the couples treatment field—specifically John Welwood, John Gottman, and David Schnarch—that marriage is the venue where growth and development of an individual adult continues. It is a novel way of thinking about developmental stages and the purpose of marriage.

Perhaps it will be clearer if we begin by thinking about parenting's primary role. In a young family, conscientious parents are aware that providing a nurturing environment for the children's optimum emotional and intellectual growth and development is a paramount objective of good parenting.

What is new and relevant from recent brain research is that emotional and intellectual development begins with conception and does not end with the onset of adulthood. The brain doesn't fully mature until the late thirties or mid-forties, and continues into elder years for seniors who are intentional about continuing to learn and grow.

For the majority of the population, brain development necessarily continues in the context of marriage. It is interesting to note this age coincides with the infamous "mid-life crisis" in men, and the age that many women move away from the stay-at-home mom role and return to school, the workforce or career. Not surprisingly, the mid-life time period also shows a substantial spike in divorce rates.

The environment for optimum emotional growth in adults is the same as for children…loving, appreciative, supportive, and secure. On the other side of the coin, an unsupportive, critical, and conflicted atmosphere is as dangerous for adults as it is for children.

Think of the implications! You don't automatically outgrow or adjust to the damaging effects of growing up in a negative emotional environment. Nor do you thrive in an unsupportive emotional environment as an adult, whether in the workplace or the home. Providing a supportive and encouraging atmosphere for each partner's continued intellectual and emotional growth should be a priority in a good marriage.

In fact, recent research indicates that as the Baby Boomer generation ages and health care costs skyrocket, there is spiraling emphasis on keeping people healthy throughout their ever-increasing lifespan. Even better news is that married folks live longer, healthier, and happier lives. It seems health and happiness do indeed go together!

Significant research findings include:

- Negative emotions have an adverse impact on physical health—positive emotions promote health.

- Older folks live longer and are healthier in satisfying relationships.

- Emotional and physical health are inextricably entwined.

- Stress, frustration, and unhappiness undermine emotional well-being and physical health.

- Elders with purpose, meaningful work, and active life-styles live longer and enjoy better health.

GROWING VS. DYING

Couples break up because of decreased levels of satisfaction in the relationship...not because they stop loving each other. The results suggest that people do not end their relationship because of the disappearance of love, but because of dissatisfaction or unhappiness that develops over time, causing love to stop growing.[2]

It is the nature of living things to be either growing or dying—physically, emotionally, mentally, spiritually. Standing still is not an option. Even water that doesn't flow stagnates and no longer supports life. Stagnation is true of children, adults, and relationships as well. They are either growing or they are dying. So the subject of how to deal with the emotional and spiritual growth of marriage partners is crucial.

The emotional and physical health of the marital relationship and the family cannot be separated from each other. Honestly coming to terms with this reality is central. Convincing yourself that you can insulate children from a doomed marriage or that you can provide the necessary ingredients for the family's physical health without providing a positive and nurturing emotional environment is utter nonsense.

Much of the impetus for Dynamic Marriage comes from the fact that the divorce rate for couples of faith is the same as for the general population. The research for this book revealed clues to the reasons. The decision to commit to a spiritual path is a conscious choice. The scripts and role modeling from the family of origin are embedded long before you have the developmental ability to make such a choice. The force of embedded material outweighs conscious choice in just about every instance.

When couples have significant differences in their embedded values, it is challenging to their shared faith. One of those areas can be in regard to investing time and energy in intellectual and emotional growth. For couples who share values in these areas, it can be a major source of connection and bonding. When the role expectations and values are not in sync, it can lead to disaster. Revisiting the Johnsons' story is an example of disparity in perspectives on relationship roles and core values in these areas.

Janet came into marriage at age twenty-one with a college degree and her family's Christian beliefs and educational values. There was never much money in her family and she worked throughout high school for pocket money and bought many of her own clothes. Janet also worked several jobs to help support herself through college. She was happy growing up in a family that invested its meager disposable funds on foreign travel.

She never felt deprived or envious of wealthier friends. She viewed money as nothing more or less than the ability to buy what you really need, which, in her family, was rarely material things.

Rafe was raised in a family where both parents were second-generation immigrants and neither had a college degree. Rafe's father amassed a large personal fortune from investing in industrial property and building a successful national business. He served two terms as the popular mayor of an affluent Southern California suburban city. Dad's frequent absence and unavailability to his family was always explained as, "I'm working hard for you, so you have the things I never had."

Rafe graduated from a prestigious university with a degree in business, and like his father, traveled half the time. His growing family was not his priority, unlike Janet's dad who was immersed in family life.

Rafe and Janet were raised in the same Christian faith and felt they had everything going for them, but their embedded relationship scripts and values were profoundly different. Janet's measure of a successful person was in making a difference in the lives of others. Rafe's measure of success was in making money.

They invested two years in therapy as individuals and a couple after a crisis in their marriage and resolved many of their differences, but the core disparity in values and beliefs was never explored and addressed.

Sadly, three children and eleven years later, the marriage ended when Janet enrolled in graduate school to prepare for a career of her own. She had to make a personal choice between growing and dying; the unanticipated price was the death of her marriage and a lifetime legacy of pain for the children and regret for the parents.

The Johnsons' story illustrates a tragic ending to a promising relationship that is far too common. *Discovering a Dynamic*

Marriage is designed to prevent this demise from occurring in your relationship and the lives of other couples.

In hindsight, a divorce should never have been the ending. In spite of core differences in values in their families of origin, Janet and Rafe had many of the factors that predict success in marriage. Had Janet and Rafe been encouraged to examine the differences in their embedded scripts and values and had they made intentional choices to develop their own relationship and lifestyle values, they could have been celebrating their fiftieth anniversary together, surrounded by children and grandchildren.

GETTING ON THE SAME PAGE

The factors encompassed in intellectual development and emotional well-being may include a variety of practices: counseling, education, training, learning opportunities, etc. Many times, a spouse may feel threatened and fear being shut out, outgrown, or left behind.

In fact, the threat may be real. When one spouse has made a serious commitment to emotional growth or therapy in which the partner is not involved, a genuine danger of a disconnect exists. This danger is particularly true if the non-involved partner assumes a closed-heart stance that is resistant or disparaging of the process. In this case, the spouse undertaking personal growth may be reluctant to share the journey, and ultimately, move away from the partner.

One spouse undertaking a course of study for a new career or career advancement can also be threatening to the other partner. Humans as a species are resistant to change, especially when they feel the changes are required by another's decisions or goals. This is an example of a "forced-choice" decision discussed in the chapter on conflict.

A shared commitment to support one another's growth and to stay in close communication through any growth or change process by a partner can enrich the marriage. Using a sports metaphor, a healthy relationship passes the ball back and forth like the innings in a baseball game. Each partner has his or her turn at bat while the other pitches the ball. A good marriage is an exercise in teamwork and sportsmanship.

AVOIDING THE DANGERS

Emotional and spiritual growth generally entail a level of emotional intensity and intimacy with oneself, and often another person other than the spouse, such as a teacher, mentor, coach, or friend with similar interests. Most spouses crave being the most significant person in their beloved's life.

A legacy of early attachment needs and an individual journey in self-discovery may prove threatening to a spouse who doesn't feel included. This consequence is not inevitable, however. An equal opportunity exists to use individual passions to enrich the marriage. The difference, once again, is a common commitment to inclusion, support, and communication.

A couple must explore and articulate each partner's needs in this area. It is possible the needs can be incorporated into a couple's life and processed in a way that deepens rather than destroys intimacy. People who love one another and desire a life together should never have to choose between growing themselves and loving another. It is a false dilemma. Growth and expansion in the individuals should enrich the relationship, not divide. When it divides, hidden factors are complicating the equation.

Change triggers disequilibrium in a relationship as it does in most instances. It would be nice if emotional shifts were similar to one partner undergoing a surgery that disables him or her for a predictable period of time. It completely disrupts the household routine and requires adjustment from everyone. The difference is everyone's expectations are clear; the recovery timeline, the temporary disruption, the tasks assigned. The aftermath is temporary and predictable.

The growth of individuals in a relationship rarely resembles synchronized swimming or ice dancing. It is more like two sailboats racing into the wind, tacking this way and that, one moving ahead and the other struggling to catch up, another pulling ahead with full sails and falling behind with sails flapping—powered by an unseen inner force to an unknown destination. Random winds and restless seas are inherent in relationships as in life.

An honest dialogue about each partner's feelings and needs in a spirit of love and cooperation will result in an agreement that supports each of the individuals, grows the relationship, and builds a strong and happy family. Change is inevitable. Trust yourself, your beloved, and your relationship and keep sailing whatever the wind or seas bring. Life is an adventure….Enjoy the journey.

Discussion:

Share any feelings of anxiety, reluctance, or resistance in the area of growth (yours or your partner's) with your partner.

EXERCISES

1. How would you describe your parents' relationship as: synchronized swimmers, ice dancers, or sailboats sailing into the wind?

2. Which of these images have you recreated in your relationship?

3. What longings do you have in the area of personal interests…travel, education, hobbies, recreation, career, etc.

4. Which longed for activities are solo and which can be shared?

5. Do you feel disconnected from your partner because of a personal interest, either theirs or yours?

OUR AGREEMENT ON INTELLECTUAL DEVELOPMENT & EMOTIONAL WELL-BEING

SECRET #7

SPIRITUAL & RELIGIOUS

An individual's spiritual dimension serves as his or her guidance system in life. It gives life a foundation, meaning, and purpose. It has been said that human beings are born with a "God-shaped hole" in the soul that isn't filled until a person comes to terms with it. When people run from the internal mandate to acknowledge the spiritual dimension, it is difficult to find much satisfaction with anything in life. Running away from God often results in a pattern of running away from life in a variety of intangible ways.

How you come to terms with faith is the individual journey to find God and incorporate a consistent spiritual practice in your life, whatever form that takes. Although the same religious beliefs are not required for a good marriage, when couples have similar spiritual beliefs and practices and agree on how those beliefs show up in their lives, that shared belief system provides a solid foundation for marriage that can enrich and deepen the bond.

THE ROLE OF RELIGION, SPIRITUALITY AND FAITH

As you continue your journey, you come to one of the primary motivations behind Dynamic Marriage. It has been mentioned again and again in this book: the ill-fated notion of couples who enter into a relationship believing their shared faith comes with a guarantee of a happy and successful marriage. Sadly, it isn't true, no matter how much it seems that it should be.

When a relationship doesn't turn out as a couple hopes, the partners suffer not only the confusion and shame of failure, but often a loss of faith. Somehow, a feeling arises that either God or their understanding of God has failed them. But the problem is not with God or even their faith. In fact, many religious institutions go to great lengths to provide educational and inspirational opportunities to support couples in their marriages. They offer classes, seminars, Bible studies, book discussions, etc., focused on supporting couples. Notable experts of all faiths write books and offer workshops on making relationships successful.

Why haven't these experts and their books been more effective? Why haven't they changed the appalling divorce statistic among couples with a shared faith? Why don't the workshops deliver on their promises? It seems that agreement on such a significant core value should provide the insurance they expect. Revisiting the religious background of the Johnsons' story may give some hint as to the disparity.

Janet and Rafe were each raised in the same Protestant tradition. They were both devout Christians and actively involved in church before and after their marriage. They sang in the choir, they socialized with the young marrieds group, they worked with teens in the church. In the early years, they regularly shared a devotional time together. Their relationship was intimate and happy.

After Rafe entered his father's business, he was subjected to Dad's influence on a daily basis. His family's expectations and values began to reassert their power. On the day the Johnsons' second child was born, a son and namesake of his grandfather, Rafe was promoted to the position of national Sales Manager for his father's company, which required his presence in the East Coast office every other week.

Meanwhile, Janet, with a toddler, an infant, and a new home, fell naturally into the wife and mother role according to the scripts with which she was raised. The difference was that at age twenty-three, she had to do it on her own half the time…almost like a single parent. In her family of origin, Dad was a daily and involved parental presence.

The young Johnsons felt they had everything going for them, but their embedded relationship scripts and values were in opposition. Janet's measure of a person was in making a difference in the lives of others. Rafe equated success with making money. Although they shared a faith and spiritual values, other values that gave their lives meaning were dissimilar. Rafe's regular absences also eroded their devotional time together.

This situation has been discussed before but bears repeating in this chapter on Spirituality; herein lies the answer to the enigmatic statistic. Even when partners are raised in a similar spiritual tradition, the commitment to the practice of faith is a conscious adult decision while embedded scripts learned in the classroom of the parents' marriage are unconscious. Implanted beliefs, values, and fears trump the conscious mind as long as they remain hidden beneath the seas like the iceberg that sank the *Titanic*, and tragically they sink well-intentioned and devoted couples of faith every day.

SPIRITUAL VALUES AND BELIEFS

It becomes clear that in forming a relationship, many factors contribute to or compete with a couple's love and commitment to one another. Spiritual beliefs and personal faith, as central as they are, comprise only one part of the partnership equation. When raised in the same religious tradition, an understanding exists of what God expects of individual believers and married couples. In a common faith, the tenets are known and shared. This shared understanding and belief is a powerful bond and a solid foundation for a relationship.

Relationship scripts and role expectations are deeply embedded and unknown. As a child, you absorbed whatever was the hidden truth of your parents' relationship. Although your parents may have attempted to keep unpleasant realities concealed from you and perhaps from themselves, children are tuned in to subtle nuances in the environment. Secrets take up residence in the subconscious and exert an imperceptible but profound influence on your beliefs, decisions, and relationships as adults.

When you were a child, you observed your parents' behavior and felt the hypocrisy when the observed behavior belied stated beliefs. In other words, when your parents didn't "walk the talk," you picked up on the duplicity. This hypocrisy explains why many children come into adolescence already cynical about the faith and the religious institutions in which they were raised.

This early cynicism creates several complications in forming a new relationship bond. First, when you were a child, you picked up on many things going on around you, but you had limited capacity to interpret them accurately. A common example of this perceptual distortion is returning to your childhood home and feeling surprised that it is much smaller than your memory of it. In your present home, get down on your knees and crawl around; lie on your back and look at the furniture, the ceiling, the size of the room. Notice how it must appear to an infant or toddler.

Material is stored as it was perceived by a child, not necessarily as it actually was. The same is true of emotional information and feelings; children make sense of what's going on around them with the limited understanding they have, and they record it, whether or not it is accurate. Add to that the reality of how they are totally dependent on these giants who care for them—or not—and you begin to get a glimpse of how distorted embedded scripts may be. These models are your default under pressure; they are actively in play at all times, but not accessible to update with current information.

ESTABLISHING SPIRITUAL PRACTICES

The task for you as a couple is to identify and acknowledge the forces at work in your lives—historical, spiritual, and emotional. You have to understand all of them and how they interact in order to have a successful partnership. You have to share your deeply held personal convictions in each area of your life. When you have shared your individual beliefs, you can craft a spiritual practice that is satisfying and sustaining to you both.

Perhaps you can learn from the Carters' story as Josh Carter himself tells it.

I believe that the spiritual element of a person's life is essential to keep all elements of life oiled and running well. A few years ago, my marriage was in shambles. It was almost over after thirty-eight years. Seeking to keep it from crashing into the wall, we were each in personal counseling and together in marital counseling.

As I looked at my life closer than I ever had, I saw what a mess my faith life was. I began to put it back together. A couple of key elements to get my spirituality back on track were a more attentive prayer life and a CD I found of Morning Prayer services.

Liturgy[1] gives my life meaning. I listened to a twenty-minute service of Psalms, hymns, Scripture, and prayers each morning. Darlene noticed the difference. I felt the difference. My neglected spirituality began to make a healthy recovery. As I got my spirituality in tune, I was able to pay more attention to other neglected parts of my life, especially my marriage.

It would be simplistic to say that this change alone saved my marriage. But it would also be unwise to ignore how important it was—and in fact, still is.

SPIRITUAL PURPOSE

A sense of purpose gives life meaning, and purpose is a very personal matter. Individual purpose tends to take a backseat during courtship and the early days of marriage. The new relationship with your beloved floods you and the space normally given to purpose. Love is all the purpose you need for life to have meaning in the process of forming a loving connection intended to last a lifetime.

Even if the two of you are involved in a shared spiritual practice, it is the wonder of finding love that consumes your heart and mind, as it should. Savor the early enchanted days and be grateful for them. Keep the memories alive forever. Remember the nostalgic journey in Secret #1 and celebrate your love story always in your romantic moments together.

All too often, in the settling into a life of couplehood with the challenges and demands of careers and parenthood, purpose becomes centered around tangible things rather than personal meaning and soul care. It is difficult to stay conscious of spiritual matters while juggling all the balls in the air. Carving out a time to retreat into solo spiritual practice, let alone together, presents a challenge.

INDIVIDUAL & SHARED SPIRITUAL PATHS

The initial step for each of you is to examine and clarify your current beliefs as individuals. Reflect on the evolution of those beliefs from your earliest awareness of God or spiritual matters to the present. Be aware that making a commitment, having children, and investing in a career have changed you.

Recall previous discussions about continuing adult development. Whatever life stage you are currently in, or the transitions you now face, you are not the person you were before. You must update your own inner perceptions of who you are before you can share your journey with one another.

When you have spent some time exploring where you have been and where you are in your faith journey, reveal it to your beloved. This is a time for respect, curiosity, and openness, not to defend your own views or to convert your partner to your way of thinking. Honor your partner's willingness to open up to you. Listen thoughtfully, reverently, and with an open heart to your partner's perspective on why he or she believes or practices a certain way.

Look for the spaces where your convictions and beliefs overlap. Explore the possibilities for developing a spiritual practice together. Prayer, meditation, music, devotions, Bible study, and private worship are all options for couples. Set aside an unhurried time that makes sense with your schedules.

Don't characterize this as another "to do" on an already crowded task list. Rather think of spiritual practice as a respite to restore and renew your soul. This special time is an invitation to God or Spirit to flow through you, your marriage, your relationships, and your life. A shared spiritual practice provides a compass for your voyage in life.

DIFFERENCES IN FAITH

When you hit a snag…pay attention to your closed-heart responses. The objective is not to agree on everything; that is unrealistic and not necessary for spiritual accord. The goal is to come to a place where you understand your partner's position, honor each other's views, and respect individual differences. The happiest couples are not those who are mirror images of one another but those who are more committed to being related than to being right.

RELIGIOUS, CULTURAL AND/OR ETHNIC DIFFERENCES

Every marriage is a cross-cultural experience in the sense that regardless of whether two individuals are from the same or different cultures, they come from different family systems that exert a powerful silent influence, as you will recall in the Johnsons' story. The family they create together is another brand new system that has never existed before. Crafting it consciously—realizing that what you create will be the FOOSA [2] your children will have to deal with in their marriages one day—puts you in the top 1 percent!

Religion and spirituality are one of the primary areas where it is tempting to require your partner to validate your right to believe the way you do by agreeing with you…in the name of God, of course! You can fall into the trap of the ends justifying the means. What could be wrong with asking your partner to share your spiritual convictions…especially since they are God's truth?

What if you feel…resistant, defensive, threatened, judgmental, blaming…? Admit your feelings openly with your partner, and dive into the discussion to discover the trigger point for you and the underlying fear. What needs are seeking to be met? Ask for patience and support in working through the situation together until you are back in an open-heart space and connection is restored. When you work together to push beyond where you would normally quit in frustration, you learn that diving into your own internal world actually succeeds.

Remember that fear, not conflict, is the real threat. Fear consumes you when you don't have an effective model for resolving conflict without damage to each other and the relationship. Conflict is inevitable in human relationships. The realm of spiritual and religious convictions can be a prime trigger point for conflict in some couples. *It is possible to have success in containing conflict and growing from it.*

EXAMPLES OF SPIRITUAL PRACTICES NOT CONNECTED TO A RELIGIOUS INSTITUTION

- Meditation

- Yoga

- Martial Arts

- Silent Retreats

- Wilderness experiences: hiking, camping, kayaking

- Intentional writing: journaling, diaries, poetry, automatic writing

SECULAR ACTIVITIES BASED ON CONVICTIONS AND BELIEFS

Couples often bond around a secular cause or conviction they both hold. Outside of a religious community, a few activities you can engage in and financially support are:

- Politics

- Protests

- Fundraising

- Volunteering

- Charitable causes

- Education

- Art and music

- Children

- Poverty

- Health

- Public policy

Spending time together in such activities adds depth and dimension to a relationship. Friendships develop with other couples who share this particular interest, but may come from a different religious community, expanding you as individuals and as a couple. Involving your children in these types of activities teaches them about the joy of giving to others and the rewards of contributing to the good of the community.

EXERCISE

Answer the questions individually and then come together for discussion.

1. Examine the Values agreement from Secret #2.

2. Which values align with your spiritual beliefs?

3. Identify any values in conflict with your spiritual beliefs.

4. What can you do to realign them to promote greater congruence?

5. List your past and current spiritual practices as individuals and as a couple.

Discussion:

Answer the questions individually and then come together for discussion.

1. How do the religious and spiritual views you were raised with impact your adult values?

2. At one point, did this awareness result in a "conversion" decision or experience?

3. What is your preferred spiritual practice today?

4. What spiritually-based character traits do you value in yourself…in your spouse?

5. Which of these spiritual values/traits inspire and sustain an environment of trust in your relationship?

6. What spiritual values/traits do you look for in others with whom you are closely associated?

7. What spiritual practices have you found satisfying in the past? When?

8. Are you still actively engaged?

9. What led to your abandoning them?

10. Would they be meaningful to you now?

11. Make a list of spiritual practices you would like to share with your beloved.

12. Discover, appreciate, and celebrate the areas of agreement.

13. What have you discovered about the internal landscape of your partner?

14. Look for the common ground in the areas where your views are different.

OUR AGREEMENT ON SPIRITUAL & RELIGIOUS BELIEFS AND PRACTICES

RICHES & RESOURCES

Part III: Riches & Resources

PROLOGUE

Discovering a Dynamic Marriage is intentionally designed to inspire you to think about marriage in a new way. In every chapter, you have explored how your embedded scripts and role expectations have determined your relationship behaviors and sabotaged your best intentions. The way to diminish the power of subliminal material is to examine what beliefs drive your behavior and consciously shift the way you were taught to think about things. A new perspective opens your mind to view matters from an alternative standpoint, freeing you and your beloved to break out of old patterns and design new ones together, starting with a clean slate.

In review, *Discovering a Dynamic Marriage* encourages a new perspective by setting up categories in which to group the twelve areas of marriage. In Part I, we set the Four Compass Points, kicking off the process of differentiation and establishing a framework for learning new relationship skills. Thus empowered, you take ownership of your marriage and realize the dreams you have for your relationship. The focus is on *who you are* as an individual and *how you relate* in a relationship.

Part II focused on you and your partner becoming physically, emotionally, and spiritually healthy, mature adults capable of a deep, committed relationship. You discovered who you are as an individual and what work you have to undertake to become the person you want to be.

In Part III, you will look at the areas requiring many of the "forced choice" dilemmas that couples must face. Riches & Resources concentrates on what you have, and what you are willing to give to accumulate it and keep it. Time and energy are the resources we have to offer in exchange for the "stuff" that makes us feel comfortable and satisfied. Material things require an investment of time, energy, and/or money. These decisions necessitate profound conversations about values and priorities regarding what really matters to you as individuals and as a couple.

Secret #8: Work, Careers & Business is where your investment of time and energy generates the money to finance your lifestyle. This area of marriage has changed so dramatically in the past fifty years that no operational role-definitions are established. It may be that a world providing static role expectations is a thing of the past. Until the past half-century, work and career were primarily a man's world. Two-career, two-income families are now the norm in middle class households with two adults. Many homes are single-parent families with only one income.

Today couplehood is a minefield couples must navigate according to their individual needs, values, and temperaments.

The world is changing so rapidly that the basic preparation for marriage, as in everything, is self-knowledge, flexibility, and skills for identifying and managing discontinuous change. The skills required for a successful marriage are the same skills needed for effective parenting and relationships in all areas of life. In today's business climate, the emphasis is on leadership and team-building. If you consider your partner and you to be a team with good leadership skills, your marriage, career and parenting will improve commensurately.

When couples are in business together, additional stresses are placed on the marriage. It is highly advisable to retain the guidance of a coach or therapist specializing in family businesses. You have the benefit of their experience with the successful strategies of many other couples facing similar challenges. It is well worth the investment.

Secret #9: Finances & Money focuses on revealing each partner's scripts about money, and even more importantly, the meaning of money to each of you. In most cases of recurring conflict over money, the issue that causes the most difficulty is usually not what you think it is. Generally, doing a FOOSA reveals that the messages you have about money from your family of origin are different, and the meaning of money is not the same for each of you. The Exercise and Discussion section at the chapter's end will guide you to some insights that will help you navigate stormy financial seas.

Secret #10. Leisure Time is a concept that couples rarely think to discuss. Europeans take their leisure much more seriously than Americans do. We are largely raised with the concept of hard work to the exclusion of any importance being credited to leisure activities. In this chapter, you will consider the fact that it is in leisure time that the most precious and memorable moments of our lives with our loved ones occur. Allotting sufficient riches and resources to honor this is an essential segment of your agreement. Budget the time and money for magic to happen in your life!

OUR GOALS FOR PART III: RICHES & RESOURCES

SECRET #8

WORK, CAREERS & BUSINESS

Riches & Resources is the category where unacknowledged and/or unresolved power and control issues are most likely to combine to cause the perfect storm. Later in this chapter, you will learn that work and careers are deeply entwined with your personal identity and self-worth for reasons we will explore in some detail.

But for now, we will begin with a history of economic and social changes resulting in growing numbers of women entering the workplace, which in turn forced shifts in marriage roles and expectations. Women, usually unmarried or widowed, had often worked, but mainly in service or apparel-related industries. The advent of large numbers of women into the regular male-dominated workforce began during World War II. The military commandeered young men into the services so women took their places in factories producing goods for the war machine.

THE LEGACY OF A WORLD AT WAR

Returning home from the war, the men were confronted with a completely different type of woman than had existed before the war. Women had become self-supporting and self-reliant. They were accustomed to making their own money and their own decisions on how to spend both their time and their money. They had no intention of giving up their newfound autonomy and maturity. But the war-fueled factory jobs were drying up, and returning vets needed what employment was available. Women were filled with frustration and discontent.

Men came home expecting life to pick up where it had left off for them. The metamorphosis of the women in their life came as a shock. The yearning for the home and relationship they had left behind was the vision that had kept them alive in the trenches. Now they found it no longer existed. Already in shock from the experience of combat, the lack of the anticipated comfort and relief men expected on their return home was disappointing. They felt displaced, confused, and angry.

As stressful as combat was, the war provided men with a sense of purpose and belonging to a brotherhood with a clear mission and objective. That too was lost and a meaningful job to replace the lost mission and camaraderie was not forthcoming. All the things that defined a man to himself were stripped away.

This generation of men and women, forced to adjust to a whole new definition of male and female roles, gave birth to the Baby Boomers. It fell to the Baby Boomer generation to make the transition from a traditional "Father Knows Best" model of marriage to a partnership model of equals. We as a society are still navigating the tides of that transition.

As you can see from this brief history, Work & Careers is an area of marriage so dramatically changed in the past fifty years that operative role-definitions have still not been established. It may require another two decades before we have an idea of what works in our world.

Currently, it is a minefield, each couple must navigate in accordance with their individual needs, values, and personalities. The enduring and timeless principles underpinning Dynamic Marriage will empower you to survive rough seas in this area, whatever your lifestyle choices.

Keep in mind that the couple of today was most likely raised by parents or grandparents who were members of the popularly named "Baby Boomer" generation. Boomers were products of a generation that we can hardly begin to understand. Boomer women were raised in a *Leave It to Beaver* and *Father Knows Best*[1] world.

If those immensely popular television shows are unfamiliar to you, you've made the point. In the early days of television, they were the most popular family sitcoms of the 1950s. Originally on the radio, the TV show for *Father Knows Best* ran from 1954-1960 and *Leave It to Beaver* aired from 1957-1963. Everyone in the Baby Boomer generation grew up watching these shows.

Jim Anderson, the father in *Father Knows Best*, was deferred to, waited on, catered to, and no one ever questioned his God-given right to make all the family decisions because he was the "breadwinner." He was always portrayed in a shirt and tie, sitting in his designated chair after his day at work, ruling over his ever-grateful household as a wise and benign dictator. Even though he was sometimes the butt of jokes, nobody really questioned the notion that "Father knows best."

In *Father Knows Best,* Margaret, the mother, was the voice of reason, while Jim, as the father, offered wise advice to his children whenever they had problems. Jim worked as a sales-man, while Margaret was a stay-at-home mom. The family was close to ideal, serving as a model of what a family should be, but it was probably not an accurate reflection of family life for anyone, or at least, for very few.

While *I Love Lucy* and *The Honeymooners* were tongue-in-cheek parodies of marriage and family life, *Leave It to Beaver's* June Cleaver and *Father Knows Best's* Jim Anderson were role models of the ideal family to the war-baby and Boomer gen-erations who were teenagers and young children during that decade. In a 1983 interview, Billy Gray (who played "Bud") spoke disparagingly of *Father Knows Best*:

> *I wish there was some way I could tell kids not to believe it. The dialogue, the situations, the characters were all total-ly false. The show did everyone a disservice. The girls were always trained to use feminine wiles, to pretend to be helpless to attract men. The show contributed to a lot of problems between men and women we see today....I think we were all well motivated, but what we did was run a hoax. 'Father Knows Best' purported to be a reasonable facsimile of life. And the bad thing is, the model is so deceitful. It usually*

revolved around not wanting to tell the truth, either out of embarrassment, or not wanting to hurt someone. If I could say anything to make up for all the years I lent myself to that, it would be, 'You Know Best.'

In *Leave It to Beaver*, June Cleaver was ten-year-old Beaver's apron-wearing, cookie-baking mother—always in a dress, fully made-up, freshly coiffed from her weekly visit to the salon, wearing high-heel pumps even in the kitchen, of course. From the show, you would assume she had nothing better to do than attend to her family's every whim. She had no personal identity, needs, or feelings outside the wife/ mother role. She certainly did not have a job, let alone a career.

June Cleaver defined the perfect wife and mother for an entire Baby Boomer generation of women, and shaped the role expectations of men. But it was a dying role in a changing world.

Leave It to Beaver has attained an iconic status in the United States with the Cleavers exemplifying the idealized suburban family of the 1950s. It is a coming-of-age tale for white, middle class boyhood of the time. In a typical episode, Beaver would get into some sort of trouble, then have to face his parents who would gently reprimand him and show him how to change his behavior or solve his dilemma.

Education (for men), occupation, marriage, and family are presented in *Leave It to Beaver* as requirements for happiness. The father, Ward, is an educated professional with a steady office job while June is happy caring for the home and children. Marriage is held up as the cornerstone for happiness among the middle class. Ward and June are also models of late-1950s conscientious parenting. Stay-at-home June maintains a loving, nurturing home, and Ward supervises the behavior and moral education of his sons in a consistent fashion.

THE ROLE OF WOMEN

At the time of these television programs, if a woman wanted to break out of established roles and get a job, let alone a career, she had to fight not only a husband's resistance in the home but also compete in a hostile male-dominated environment in the workplace. Even if working full-time, women were expected to fulfill all the responsibilities and expectations of the stay-at-home wife and mother.

It was unthinkable for a man raised in the June and Jim generation to help with household chores or child-rearing duties other than deciding and dispensing punishment and money. Mowing the lawn, household repairs, and washing the car were the primary prescribed domestic duties of a husband/father in the Baby Boomer generation. After all, he worked all day!

You might be wondering why we are spending so much time reviewing the history relevant to this chapter? By now, you are familiar with the process of examining the roots of beliefs and behaviors that may cause problems in your relationships and in your life. In the process of digging into the past and deciphering the embedded scripts, the tendency is to fall into the trap of blaming parents for everything. Blaming anyone for the issues in your life is a way of shirking responsibility. One benefit of understanding the roots of your scripts is to be gentle and forgiving of yourself, not angry, resentful and disrespectful of your parents.

Young children tend to be curious about their parents' lives, but this curiosity disappears with the self-absorption of adolescence. The result is that you come into marriage with an image of your parents that probably hasn't been updated since you entered your teens. Think of how much you have changed in the ensuing years. Isn't it possible your parents have changed as well? Your memories of your parents shaped who you are, but your perceptions were necessarily distorted by your age, dependency and developmental level.

Dynamic Marriage is dedicated to vitality in all your relationships. Specifically in the matter of work and careers, having insight into the role models your parents and grandparents dealt with helps you understand your entire family history.

Updating and correcting your perceptions about who they were then, and who they are now, is one of the significant steps. Become curious about them, check out the accuracy of your important memories, especially those that wounded or frightened you, or left you with negative messages about your worthiness, lovability or adequacy.

The objective of your inquiry is not to make them understand you, but for you to understand yourself and how you came to be who you are. Approach these crucial conversations *with curiosity and intention to appreciate and understand* the people who wrote the scripts that drive your beliefs and behaviors, and in this context, your embedded scripts about relationships.

THE CROWDED BED

Many years ago, there was a book cover showing a young couple lying in the middle of a giant bed with a middle-aged couple lying on either side. There's truth in that picture! At least six people are in a marriage—the young couple and each set of parents. Finding out who they are and what makes them tick deepens your understanding of yourself and expedites the differentiation process.

What expands you as an individual increases your capacity for intimacy. Keep this objective in mind as you delve further into the roles that molded the generations before you.

The rules changed during the quarter century that Baby Boomers were raising families. Women of that era were role-locked and had to hack their way through the barriers however they could. The children were the audience of mother's flailing around trying to figure it out, when the goalpost was in fog and always moving. It wasn't always ladylike and graceful.

As frustrating and confusing as it was for mothers, it had to be terrifying for their children, especially daughters. They— as we all do—needed mothers who were grounded and secure in their roles.

Some Boomer women—the pioneers—couldn't settle for the status quo. They were the first generation of women earning college degrees in growing numbers. Most of these women were not the bra burners of the militant feminist variety[2], but they felt the ground shifting beneath them, stirring some whispered dream of equality and freedom they couldn't silence.

Other women in the Baby Boomer generation remained content to spend their days baking cookies and playing bridge, blissfully out of the fray in a dying June Cleaver world. Perhaps their daughters are better for it; we can't know. But the doors that swung open to all the daughters of following generations are doors the pioneers crashed through with a sledgehammer or whatever means they had at hand.

At the same time that this major shift was going on among women, men were losing their long established roles as head of the household—the breadwinner, the authority figure, the leader. While women have made significant, much-needed strides in their positions in the world and the work force, many men have not yet figured out what an authentic male role is and where they fit into the new scheme of things.

In the Baby Boomer generation, a man's entire self-concept revolved around his ability to support his family. Whether white collar or blue collar, his work was the primary source of his identity. When men are introduced to one another, they typically ask, "What do you do?" Even retired men ask, "How did you make a living?"

The work a man does is not only how he defines himself, but how he registers other men in his internal catalogue. In the Baby Boomer generation, work did and still does define largely who men are to themselves and each other. Great pride was taken in the ability to earn the income that supported a family and household.

When women began entering the work force in growing numbers, this distinction began to erode. Men felt displaced and left without a clear definition of a significant role in life and family. Society in flux offered no compass to chart a man's course through the changing tides. Economic factors were beyond anyone's control, regardless of gender, but they had a profound effect on male roles, feelings of self-worth and identity during this transitional generation we call Baby Boomers.

Today, with households dependent upon two incomes and still barely able to survive, both men and women derive their self-esteem from being successful at the things they value. Generally, the top of the value list is God, marriage, family, and career. But finding a balance is a continually stressful juggling act in terms of time, money, and energy referred to as "Riches & Resources."

Crucial factors weave the tapestry of your personal identity, beliefs, values, and role expectations, out of which you weave the fabric of your intimate relationships. These factors exert a silent but powerful influence framing your expectations of the role a partner should fulfill. If your father was the bread-winner and mom was a stay-at-home housewife and mother, you come into marriage with a certain set of role expecta-tions. If your mother was a career woman or worked full-time, you have a different role model.

If each partner had a very different family configuration in the area of work and careers, getting clear about the expec-tations you have as a result is crucial. Without this knowl-edge, you are at the mercy of the silent forces dictating your expectations and the future you envision. A journey into the past empowers you to chart a course for the future together. Think about this: if you aren't the captain of your own life, someone else is….It's your choice.

The driving force at the core of conflict in this area—as in many others—is the struggle for power and control. What you want to strive for as the driving force is fairness and equality and mutually valuing the contribution of each to your family's health and welfare. It is crucial to review your Values Agreement here to make sure that earning power doesn't trump other significant contributions that align with your agreed to values. The Starks have a successful fifty-year marriage. Let's take a look at how the Starks handled these issues in the years they were raising a family:

Ted and Connie started dating at Stanford University even though they were raised in the same affluent suburban community. They married after both graduated and Ted had completed one year of his three year stint as a naval officer and Connie attended a year of graduate school. They waited to have their two daughters until Ted completed his tour of duty. Ted went to work for a major aerospace company headquartered near their hometown. Connie was a full-time stay at home mom. From the beginning Ted—whose parents divorced when he was 13—considered Connie's job the most significant, his was just a means to fund the operation, but the family was what mattered to both of them.

He was aware that Connie missed the stimulation of adult company and pursuits. He insisted on her taking a weekend day to meet with girlfriends, take a class, attend a seminar, shop or whatever she needed to do for herself. When she was housebound because the kids were sick, he sent her out in the evening and took over nurse duties. Connie didn't resume working until the girls were in high school. In the summer she taught children to swim in a pool especially built for this purpose. They lived the values they adopted when they married.

Couples may agree to these values in theory, but in practice, the silent, unconscious forces remain at the helm, undermining best intentions. Lack of awareness, inadequate differentiation, and maladaptive life strategies developed to cope with disappointing childhood experiences fuel the struggle for power and control.

When partners are not clear about core power and control issues, any attempt at resolution is stalled. If you allow problem-solving to degenerate into a power struggle, the conflict is unlikely to be on target to reach a satisfactory solution. Your goal as a couple is to come to a joint decision about how you want to function in regard to the work and career area of your marriage. Begin with a visit to your individual role-models for marriage—your parents' marriage—review your values, keep an open heart, and listen lovingly to one another's needs and wants as an individual and in your relationship.

EXERCISES

1. What family of origin role expectations did you carry into your marriage.

2. How have those expectations caused conflict in this area.

   a. How will what you have learned in this chapter impact the conflict?

   b. How can it be resolved?

3. What would you like your children to know regarding this area of marriage?

Discussion:

1. What role did your parents have in the area of work Full time? Part time? Stay at home?

2. What was your expectation of your spouse when you came into the marriage?

3. Did one of you expect to be the full time bread winner?

4. Do you still have vestiges of the belief that the money earner has the most important job?

OUR AGREEMENT ON WORK, CAREERS & BUSINESS

FINANCES & MONEY

This chapter probably will not be what you expect. Hopefully, that's been true of many chapters—as they have taken unexpected turns and stirred up questions that made you think from a new perspective and search for entirely new answers to old, familiar issues.

Adding to the complications and clouding the lines of the money issue in a marriage are idealistic hopes that your relationship and sufficient financial resources will put an end to all losses and longings from the past…and insulate you from them in the present. Money is a difficult enough subject on its own, but when burdened with the expectation of happiness it is further obscured by emotional undercurrents and lack of awareness about what money really represents for you. Keeping money as a separate issue with distinct boundaries is challenging work.

One of the objectives of *Dynamic Marriage* is to challenge you to break out of naive expectations and default strategies. This goal is particularly essential in the area of money. So, this chapter about money and financial matters will be less about how to negotiate a budget than to uncover the roots of conflict over money which is generally differences in the meaning of money to each of you.

You will then sort through and discover what is still true for each of you, what is realistic, and what is consistent with your current values and priorities. Equipped with a full knowledge of your own unique perspectives, values, and needs, you can chart your own course through the turbulent waters of financial seas. Remember, if you aren't the captain of your ship, someone else is!

Money and financial matters top the list of conflicted subjects in any partnership. This situation is especially true in marriage where the partners come into a relationship with two entirely different histories, sets of traditions, emotional scripts, and expectations. What if you approached money with the understanding that it doesn't need to be any more difficult in a marriage than any of the other subjects you have successfully negotiated?

The most important aspect of the sorting-out process is tuning into your heart's murmurings over the din of the world in order to discern the meaning of success in your own life. To discover what makes you happy. To learn what gives your life purpose and meaning. To join forces in designing the financial future that supports the lifestyle you both desire.

To begin the journey, we will recap a brief history of the message perpetuated by our society that has shaped our beliefs and aspirations about money and success. Understanding this message is important because none of us is immune to the media's onslaught and the economic pressures regarding what constitutes achievement or success in our society.

THE GIFT AND BURDEN OF THE AMERICAN DREAM

As a nation, we Americans predominately measure success in terms of the accumulation of money and material possessions in the pursuit of status, affluence, and security. What is commonly referred to as the "American Dream" originated from the viewpoint of immigrants who were attracted to the New World by a promise of freedom and a set of ideals that included opportunities for prosperity, success, and upward mobility achieved through hard work.

The idea of the American Dream was rooted in the United States Declaration of Independence that proclaimed "all men are created equal" and "endowed by their Creator with certain inalienable Rights" including "Life, Liberty and the pursuit of Happiness." To those in societies with centuries of oppression and restrictions limiting people according to their class, caste, religion, race, or ethnicity, this description sounded like the Promised Land indeed.

For a fortunate few, America lived up to the promise; for the majority, freedom and hard work materialized, but wealth and security remained a dream.

The American Dream, which lured tens of millions from all nations to our shores over three centuries, has not exclusively been a dream of material plenty, although that has doubtlessly counted heavily. More than that, it was a dream of the freedom to grow to full potential as men and women. It was a dream that simple human beings of any and every stripe could grow unhampered by barriers and social orders that existed in older civilizations for the benefit and protection of a class hierarchy.

Following a century of prosperity and westward expansion, the ethos of the American Dream dimmed with the Great Depression. President Franklin D. Roosevelt was instrumental in resurrecting the ideal to inspire hope in the citizenry with the promise of home ownership and a "car in every garage." It was a modest dream intended to motivate the average American. The consumerism culture that has since evolved has recast the American Dream to represent a lavish home in a prestigious neighborhood and an expensive car for every family member over sixteen. At what cost?

One author[1] identifies four American Dreams that promoted the consumer culture.

1. Abundance: Material possessions give us pride in being a prosperous family in the richest society on earth.

2. Democracy of goods: Everyone has access to goods regardless of race, gender, ethnicity, or class in contrast to societies where only the privileged have access to luxury.

3. Freedom of choice: An expanding variety of goods allows people to create their own lifestyle.

4. Novelty: Ever-changing fashions, the latest models, and new products whet the voracious consumer appetite for novelty. This trend—or addiction—has given

rise to "planned obsolescence" and "keeping up with the Joneses."

To initiate a discussion on money with your partner, try out this shift in perception. Armed with awareness of the perpetual media onslaught, think about the ways you are caught in the tide of consumerism. How do you *buy in*—literally and figuratively? What does it cost you financially, physically, and emotionally? If you cleared out your closets, house, garage, (and storage unit) of everything you don't need or use, what size home would you require? If you added up the cost of everything you cleared out (don't forget the savings on the storage unit!), how much could you put in savings?

If the cars you drive were chosen to be simply efficient, safe, and reliable—not status symbols, how much would you save? If you added up all the savings, how many more irreplaceable hours could you spend with people you love and on worthwhile and/or philanthropic activities? How many less hours could you work and still make ends meet? Figure out what you earn in an hour. When you are contemplating a non-essential purchase, calculate how many hours you have to work to own it. Is that how you prefer to spend those precious hours?

TAKING CONTROL OF YOUR OWN LIFE

Earlier, we discussed the idea that security is an illusion and unworthy to stand as a meaningful life goal. Certainly, you should responsibly plan ahead by providing an emergency fund and having a retirement strategy. However, it is an illusion that money is all it takes to be secure. When you consider the things that matter most to you—your values and priorities, what can you really protect with money? The following oft-quoted passage from the well-known Sermon on the Mount is an eye-opening concept in terms of the financial ideals we learn growing up in our society.

> *Therefore I tell you, do not worry about your life, what you will eat or what you will drink, or about your body, what you will wear. Is not life more than food, and the body more than clothing?*

> *Look at the birds of the air; they neither sow nor reap nor gather into barns, and yet your heavenly Father feeds them. Are you not of more value than they?*

> *And why do you worry about clothing? Consider the lilies of the field, how they grow; they neither toil nor spin, yet I tell you, even Solomon in all his glory was not clothed like one of these.*

> *But if God so clothes the flowers of the field, which is alive today and tomorrow is thrown into the oven, will he not much more clothe you—you of little faith?*

> *Therefore do not worry, saying, "What will we eat?" or "What will we drink?" or "What will we wear?"*

> *…your heavenly Father knows that you need all these things. So do not worry about tomorrow, for tomorrow will bring worries of its own. Today's trouble is enough for today.* (Matthew 6:25-34)

As you consider your agreement in the area of money, rethink your preoccupation with security. Most people in Western culture spend the majority of their riches and resources supporting lifestyle and security. Budgets and financial strategies revolve around maintaining lifestyle and security. Recent economic events on a global scale have revealed that economic security is ephemeral.

Anyone who has lost a job, a chunk of retirement funds in the stock market, their savings, a business, or their home, due to circumstances beyond their control—knows that economic security can disappear overnight. Anyone who has lost a loved one to illness, violence, or accident knows that protecting a loved one is impossible.

So if concentrating on riches and resources for security is futile…how do you set priorities? What is worthy of value? Your agreement on money will establish guidelines to inform financial decisions and provide the frame for the disposition and investment of family resources.

MARRIAGE AS A BUSINESS

For the majority of young couples, the only business model you have is the family you grew up in. Whether you disapprove of the way your parents handled money or you subscribe to their model, it is your default position, and your partner's is likely very different. Ambivalence or lack of clarity in this area can result in confusion and conflict. Thinking of marriage as a small business, a concept introduced earlier in this book, provides objectivity and helps to separate financial matters from emotional baggage.

The entire area of riches and resources is likely to trigger power and control issues. Money is frequently the primary battleground of a marriage. Marriage is the only business entered into with romantic notions (read hormones/phero-mones) at the helm. It is not founded on a negotiated part-nership agreement or contract, let alone a business plan!

Romance does not provide a sound basis for business deci-sions, and yet, that's where it begins for most couples. The romantic notions recede, but the business set in motion re-mains, rudderless. In addition, when you and your partner have significant unresolved differences concerning finan-cial matters or dissimilar beliefs around money, conflict is inevitable.

If money and finances have been a recurrent source of conflict in your marriage, pay attention to the biblical injunction:

> *"For where your treasure is, there also will your heart be."*
> (Matthew 6:21)

In other words, how you allocate your riches and resources discloses what is in your heart. This is the "walk your talk" or "put your money where your mouth is" part of the financial equation. It is imperative that your agreement about money begins with a re-examination and re-affirmation of your con-tract clause about values and priorities. Do your financial pri-orities reflect your heart's intentions?

> *Then he said to them, "Be careful to guard yourselves against every kind of greed, because a person's life doesn't consist of the amount of possessions he has."*
> (Luke 12:15)

The dictionary defines greed as follows: denotes an excessive, extreme desire for something, often more than one's proper share. Greed means avid desire for gain or wealth and is definitely uncomplimentary in implication: *His greed drove him to exploit his workers.* Greediness, may refer to a craving for food; it may, however, apply to all avid desires, as in greediness *for knowledge, fame, praise.*

A recent social consciousness documentary[2] was a commentary on the predominance of greed and the eventual effects of unalloyed greed in our society. One of the poignant comparisons it made was that humans are the only living things in nature that take more than they need to thrive. Accumulating and hoarding are unknown in the natural kingdom.

Money is a metaphor for what in your life? Greed is an attempt to fill up what? We talked earlier about loss and longing as being at the bottom of most unexamined beliefs and behaviors. To what degree do your feelings and attitudes and behaviors concerning money have to do with unacknowledged and/or unresolved losses and longings?[3] What emptiness is material things attempting to fill?

Are you familiar with the following lovely phrase, which might well be a contemporary reflection on the caution expressed in the passage above from Luke?

"Life is not measured by the number of breaths we take,
but the moments that take your breath away!"
— Hilary Cooper

Has money or any other possession ever left you breathless, delighted your heart, or brought tears of joy to your eyes? What has? That's where your treasure lies!

MONEY TALK

Review your previous agreements in the Four Compass Points before proceeding. Re-affirm the newly established values and priorities you have agreed upon rather than falling back into default positions. Move into the discussion from a position of two conscientious business partners with the intention of making wise decisions about the family business.

Discussions that begin to go sideways indicate that something old has been triggered. The triggered person is no longer able to be objective. But remember, it only takes one person to step out of the old script and de-escalate the potential conflict. The untriggered partner's responsibility to the discussion's integrity is to refuse to voice the next expected line in the familiar but dysfunctional script.

Instead, a response as simple as, "I never looked at it that way," or "you make an interesting point," or "I need some time to think about that." This communication technique is called "moving from content to process."

When a conversation starts to go off track, process refers to the practice of curiosity (discovery): "What are we really talking about?" "What just happened?" "What just got triggered?" "Are we still talking about _____?" Never engage in or continue conversations that deteriorate into personal, hurtful attacks on one another. Suggesting a delay in the discussion until you are both in a better place for the sake of safety and integrity in the relationship is not the same thing as withdrawal as a power/control tactic.

There is a huge difference in motivation between calling a timeout because continuing will hurt the relationship and walking away because it isn't going the way you want. A partner will know the difference, and if it is a manipulation, it will damage trust! At the point in a disagreement that you start blaming, making personal attacks, or feeling stuck, someone needs to call "time out." Table the discussion (content) and talk about what's really going on at the feeling level (process).

> ***Money is not important enough to damage a relationship…not ever!***

A NEW PERSPECTIVE

Seeing money in its proper light eliminates most of the conflict. According to the Scriptures, money was never meant to be accumulated; it is designed as a convenient method for exchange of energy and goods, nothing else. Think of money as a river flowing by—out of which each person takes what he or she needs and allows the river to continue flowing to others to take what they need.

Consider the sun's energy that gives the planet light and nourishment or the moon and stars signaling a time for rest. None of these resources necessary for life can be accumulated and used to control others or ensure personal security. They are God's gifts to all creation.

Successfully navigating financial issues requires a mature sense of self in each partner and a solid foundation of trust between partners. To build trust in the area of finances and money, revisit the concepts of fairness and equality. The contribution of the partner who manages family affairs, nurtures children, sees to household chores, maintains health care, does scheduling, chauffeuring, etc., is at least as significant as the partner earning money.

Equally important in partnership and trust is making sure each partner's earning ability does not establish the basis for voting rights in the relationship. Many outside forces influence the earning ability of an individual and they should never be an indicator of personal worth. A person who happens to earn more or amass huge amounts of money is not superior or more valuable than the person who raises children, teaches school, works for a non-profit, cleans houses, mows lawns, or volunteers time to help the less fortunate.

DISCOVERING HIDDEN MESSAGES

How money is handled is a potentially emotional issue in the Riches & Resources category. Very often, delving into conflict over sources and ownership of money will reveal loads of significant information that is useful to the relationship. Money is a metaphor for many unrelated things. The Havens' story is a profound example.

> *Janelle did not get a substantial monthly paycheck like her husband Dan. She was self-employed and her clients paid her by the hour for her coaching and consulting time. Her habit was to deposit all the checks at the end of each week in a separate checking account. Her husband took issue with her separate account. He reasoned that his check went into the joint account and her checks should as well.*

> *Whenever the issue was raised, Janelle explained that it was important for her to see the amount build up in her account over the month so she had tangible evidence of her total earnings, and therefore, her productivity and self-esteem. If*

she were to deposit in the joint account, it felt like her contribution just "dribbled in and disappeared." At the beginning of the month, she paid her business-related expenses and then wrote a check to the joint account for an amount that was clearly a material contribution. Dan seemed to understand rationally, but his uneasy feelings persisted.

When Dan and Janelle finally seriously explored the roots of Dan's emotional response, it was revealed that when he had been in the army for two years following graduation from high school, he'd had his paychecks sent to his mother with the understanding that she would deposit them in his savings account.

When he returned home after his tour of duty, he expected to have a nest egg to hold him over until he found a job that enable him to get his own place. He discovered that his mother, who was an alcoholic, had not deposited the money in his savings account, but spent it herself and refused to acknowledge any wrongdoing.

This revelation brought immediate insight, understanding, and compassion to the issue. How could he feel otherwise in view of this history? Janelle and Dan were able to come to an agreement about their accounting procedures and put an end to conflict on this front. Their exploration also brought clarity to a number of trust issues and fears that Dan had about being taken advantage of by women.

Individual partners need to have an equal voice in the handling of money in the relationship. When there is irrational resistance to this, there are hidden forces at work. It is well worth the exploration as the Havens' experience illustrates.

PERSONAL MONEY

Partners each need to have some personal money over which they have total discretion. Things normally listed in the discretionary money category include: clothing budget, personal grooming, beauty products, hobby/craft supplies, fitness expenses, individual recreation activities, etc. You may have additional items that are specific to you and your lifestyle.

People rarely are in total agreement over the expenditure of money; it is the most frequent source of marital conflict. An element that requires agreement between you in drafting your financial contract is the amount of money each partner has for individual use. Given that money is usually in limited supply, power and control issues—with all their convoluted beliefs, values, and motives—come into play.

Money is a metaphor—cloudy, convoluted, complicated. What does money represent for each of you? Freedom emanates from understanding how you came to hold your beliefs about time, energy, money, and the values guiding your decisions about riches and resources. Discover, define, and design an agreement together that reflects the beliefs and values of your unique relationship.

PUTTING IT ALL IN PERSPECTIVE

This tragic story of what occurred in an all-American neighborhood is a poignant illustration how unimportant riches become when compared to the value of a human life.

The young families along a block in an affluent California suburb had a Memorial Day tradition to which they all looked forward. It was a combination block party, progressive potluck dinner, and food court. They all moved their deck chairs and tables from their backyards to the front. Each family prepared a dinner. The adults visited with each other while the children played games. Everyone toured each family's offerings and made their food selections. It was like a block-long potluck or food court!

This particular Memorial Day, a six-year-old daughter ran in the house to get more cake. Her older brother missed her and finally went to see what was taking so long. He noticed the back door to the pool yard standing open. He discovered his little sister floating face-down in the swimming pool. The entire block was devastated, grieving the child's untimely death. They were all painfully aware it could have happened to any one of them.

All these families had the advantages of an upper-middle-class lifestyle. They owned impressive homes, drove luxury cars, and enjoyed expensive vacations. They had 401ks and college funds for their kids' futures. They were living the hallmarks of the "American Dream."

They had achieved success and security according to the common definition. But not one family in that whole community wouldn't have given it all up to restore that one child to her family. In the years to come, imagine what Memorial Day will mean to every child and adult in that privileged neighborhood.

IN SUMMARY

What will you do differently in regards to the people you love? How will that shift change your values and priorities? What decisions will you make regarding the riches and resources you have and will have? How will you allocate time, energy, and money? These are the questions you as individuals and as a couple have to answer before you make decisions guiding your agreement on money and finances.

Take time to go through the process of discovering and defining before you embark on crafting this clause of your agreement. Adopt a practice of asking when a conversation starts to go off track…"Time out! What are we really talking about?" "What just happened?" "Where did that come from?" "Are we still talking about _____?" The discovery work you do here will provide a foundation for the next task.

EXERCISES

1. Both of you, individually, make a budget of how you would spend a million dollars if you had an unexpected windfall.

    a. What do the differences indicate in the priorities of each partner? This is a good opportunity to practice listening with *curiosity and intention to appreciate and understand.*

2. Imagine that changing just one thing would put an end to conflict over money in your relationship. What is the one thing you would change? How would you change it? How would it improve your relationship?

3. On a scale of 1 to 10, how important is money to you? To your partner?

4. What does money mean to you? To your partner?

5. Where does money fit into your values?

Discussion:

To gain insight into your current relationship's history with money, consider these questions:

1. How did your family view money when you were growing up?

2. What messages do you carry with you into the present?

3. How does it show up in:

    a.   your feelings about yourself?

    b.   your relationship with money now?

4.   Did your parents fight about money?

5.   Who generally prevailed? Why?

6.   Which parent gave in? Why?

7.   What were the power and control tactics of each of your parents?

8.   How did you as a child feel when your parents were fighting about money?

Summary:

What is the most important thing you have learned from this chapter that you want to include in your agreement?

OUR AGREEMENT ON FINANCES & MONEY

.

Secret #10

LEISURE TIME: EDUCATION, HOBBIES & RECREATION

Riches & Resources are defined as time, energy, and money. In other words, riches and resources are what you have at your disposal to spend. Work is time and energy you dedicate to generating money. Leisure is the time engaged in activities that recharge you and your relationships. Before beginning, it is important to question what you have learned about work and play as interpreted by our culture.

In the last chapter, you had a short history lesson on the American Dream. A significant aspect of the dream for the immigrants of the past was that success was the reward for hard work. In the class systems from which they came, they worked far harder than their aristocratic masters without any hope of upward mobility in their lifetimes.

So the notion that hard work could elevate their positions in life and result in success was astonishing and seductive! The problem is that today that seduction lingers, even though the latest research into successful people disproves the prevailing message.[1]

In light of this knowledge, it is critical for you as a couple to become aware of your embedded messages about success and make conscious decisions about how you want to allocate your riches and resources. It has been said that no one on his deathbed ever expressed regret about not having worked more hours. On the contrary, most people facing death regret that they didn't spend more time with the people they loved.

Working through the Exercises and Discussion questions at the end of this chapter will help increase your awareness and clarity regarding this dilemma.

OTHER CULTURES WITH DIFFERENT CRITERIA

European cultures have a very different philosophy from ours. Historically, time spent in recreation and in community with others was a priority in the upper classes. The lower classes rarely had leisure time. The privileged had no respect for the "work ethic" that dominates North American culture. In fact, a man who considered himself gentry would never admit to working. Even today, in a much more egalitarian European society, leisure continues to be much more significant than in North America. The work week is shorter, and even entry level employees have four to six weeks of "holiday" each year.

Recent research has questioned the economic efficacy of the standard forty-hour work week system in the United States. It suggests that a point of diminishing return exists in regard to the number of hours worked. It indicates the same quantity of work can be accomplished in a thirty-two-hour week without decreasing the work's quality. This information is challenging you to rethink the amount of time devoted to work. How can you carve out more quality time in activities that recharge you and revitalize your relationships?

Consider this question as an example. Do you use time more efficiently when you have a deadline? Most people do. This phenomenon is the basis of the research mentioned above. If you work four eight-hour days or five seven-hour days, you would likely accomplish an equal amount of work as in the standard forty-plus hours. It is human nature to complete a project in whatever block of time is allotted, whether three hours or eight hours. This discussion is not about turning in a sub-standard job because there isn't time to do it right. This is about maximizing efficiency when you have values that shift priorities to things other than working.

Think about what happens when you are leaving on a vacation for a week or two. You can be more productive than normal. You not only try to anticipate what needs to be completed before you leave and get it done, but you also have to anticipate what is required during your absence, and undertake preparations for the trip. If you could accomplish the same amount of work and free up six to eight hours a week, how would you invest it and with whom?

You, like most people, are driven by internalized core concepts around work, time, purpose, and the work ethic you have never scrutinized or knowingly chosen as your own. Even so, deviating from concepts tends to cause uneasiness and guilt, however irrational. These feelings are worth exploring because they could rise from outdated scripts that are not aligned with your current conscious values and priorities.

PERSONAL TIME

Most couples struggle around the issue of personal time and discretionary money at some point in their marriage. This struggle is particularly true if you neglect romantic or quality couple time for an extended period. Partners become insecure and irritable when feeling disconnected from one another. This behavior change is not necessarily evidence of fusion or lack of differentiation. Even healthy, self-referencing partners are vulnerable to an uneasy discontent from lack of contact and connection.

Insecurities may also be aroused when a partner insists on having time and money over which (s)he has complete discretion. Differing perceptions about what constitutes a relationship sometimes plays out as a demand that all leisure time should be spent in couple or family time. This position does not address the real issue. It is voicing a complaint rather than the need and longing underneath. Talking about how much you are missing close connection with your partner sounds very different from blaming him or her for being unavailable. Blame is never a productive approach to solving a problem or meeting your needs.

In the current economic climate, most marriages require two incomes just to survive. When the largest block of one or both partner's time is spent on work or income-earning pursuits, disagreement over how time is apportioned can be a source of conflict. Leisure time can be particularly problematic and a cause of strife. On the other side of the coin, if one partner is a stay-at-home caretaker, that person may crave adult company and activities and resent the earning partner spending what leisure time he or she has in solo pursuits. This negotiation can be tricky ground indeed.

If time, energy, and money are restricted resources, as they are in the majority of relationships, it constitutes a prime setup for power and control issues. The common thread in all three is limited supply. Time and energy are always limited; money is limited for all but a fortunate few. Even when money is abundant, power and control struggles may ensue over how it is to be managed and spent, and by whom.

You can begin to see how thorny this seemingly innocuous subject can be. Defining what leisure time means for you individually and as a couple encompasses all the issues explored in the Four Compass Points. How you structure leisure time begins with updating faulty beliefs, staying connected, and making choices consistent with your goals and values. Being realistic regarding available resources—time, energy, and money—is one part of the equation; the other is honoring a commitment to fairness and equality.

On the emotional front, whether or not both partners are employed, a passionate interest in individual activities may be interpreted as a personal rejection or a threat to the relationship. It is difficult to carve out quality couple time and pursue individual interests in the limited leisure time available. While couple and family demands may be legitimate, your overall objective is promoting a balanced life, well-rounded individuals, a happy marriage, and a thriving family.

Is it possible to juggle the conflicting demands and achieve these objectives? Revisit your values, goals, and priorities as a couple before you tackle a discussion on this subject. Review your agreement in Secret #6. Remind yourselves of your conversation regarding Intellectual Development and Emotional Growth. The time needed for those significant pursuits comes out of non-work time as well and must figure into the equation.

THE SIGNIFICANCE OF LEISURE TIME

Leisure time is defined as free time not allotted to work, church involvement, children's activities, family obligations, etc. It is important for individuals in an intimate relationship to engage in creative and/or recreational activities that relax, feed, and revitalize them. Personal time is spent in numerous different activities, including such solo activities as:

Fitness or Recreational: weightlifting, workouts, cycling, swimming, sailing, golf, tennis, zumba

Stress Relief: yoga, meditation, dance, singing, drama

Self-Improvement: therapy, continuing education

Hobbies: quilting, scrapbooking, jewelry making, woodworking, collecting, art/sculpture, photography, gaming, Facebook, texting, computers, writing

Partners who insist on sharing everything in order to maintain a viable marriage are unrealistic, unhealthy, and ultimately, boring. To expect the partner to fill all needs and desires is not the recipe for a successful marriage or for the individual's continued growth and development. In fact, individual pursuits add to the relationship's vitality and variety. When individuals suppress their needs for personal growth and self-expression, they build internal defenses and repress emotions. They struggle to contain loss of self-determination and longing for a sense of freedom. Denied dreams and feelings eventually become unavailable to the self or the marriage and begin to smolder and breed discontent.

Personal pursuits enrich conversations between partners when individuals share accounts of their pursuits and passions. Partners who feel secure in their connection revel in the excitement their partner enjoys in engaging in a solo interest. Negotiating this area provides an opportunity for partners to explore their dormant youthful dreams and talk about realistic ways to pursue those still alive in them.

The exploration might also bring to light unresolved childhood wounds underlying insecurities, and provide an opportunity to support one another in healing. Too often conflict and control struggles serve to exacerbate rather than alleviate these concerns, leaving the marriage more wounded in the aftermath.

Couples can discover a creative way to maximize their time for significant leisure activities that engage them both. When partners are open to looking at the internal roadblocks to healthy intimacy and sharing in the journey toward individual and relationship wholeness, they are creating the kind of "they shall be one flesh" marriage scripture describes.

FUSION AS RESISTANCE

Deep intimacy is only possible when couples dare to be open and vulnerable with one another. Part of such openness is a candid exchange of unfulfilled hopes and dreams still alive in them. A relationship at this depth requires two healthy, autonomous individuals, not clones. From the beginning, we have talked about the principle of differentiation and its relation to true intimacy. Spouses who are threatened by time spent apart are what psychologists call symbiotic or fused rather than differentiated.

Resistance to personal time requires a further exploration of the need for differentiation and the dangers of fusion. The problem in communicating about personal time has its roots in a misunderstanding about the concept of "independence" in our culture. The word is carelessly used without understanding what it means and how it undermines close relationships that still allow partners freedom to pursue individual interests. Independence and autonomy are not the same.

Independence: freedom from control, influence, support, aid, or approval of others.

You may recall visiting this concept earlier, but it bears repeating as it shows up somewhat differently in the way it applies to personal time. Independence in the context of a relationship is often interpreted as the negation of dependency needs...repression and denial is the result, which is not a health promoting state, nor an honest one. We are born with dependency needs, and we never outgrow them. What changes is our ability to meet them ourselves or decide whom we ask to meet them.

The most significant aspect in developing a healthy relationship with mutual and satisfying interdependency is trust. Anything that undermines trust is destructive to a relationship. Supporting your partner in the pursuit of personal interests requires trust and growing up.

An honest discussion and agreement between partners regarding what promotes or damages trust builds the foundation for a strong, mutually nurturing relationship. A crucial element to successfully negotiating this part of the agreement is a discussion about establishing and maintaining trust, keeping in mind the Rules and Guidelines introduced in the beginning.

> *Autonomy: freedom to choose one's actions; free will to pursue one's goals; self-regulating; self-determination; self-governing.*

Autonomy is the goal rather than independence. Autonomy is the mature adult's awareness that you have the capacity to survive on your own, but choose to share life with a beloved. The intimacy skills inherent in authentic autonomy are:

Self-control.

Staying true to your values and beliefs in the face of opposition.

Being open to the viewpoints of trusted others.

Making conscientious choices for the good of all.

Modulating emotional states—internal and external.

Being secure enough to allow the influence of others without fear of losing oneself.

PERSONAL ENERGY

Energy is less easily definable than time and money. It varies between individuals, as does the way people unwind when stressed. There are high-energy people and low-energy people, and there are differences in how they handle stress. People differ in how depleting they find the demands of necessary tasks. Health issues also factor into energy levels. Learning to be open about your limitations and respectful of the energy reserves of your partner are critical.

We've met the Starks before when they were young parents. They have managed to navigate vastly different interests and energy levels. Connie refers to Ted as a gerbil—in perpetual motion—and he affectionately calls her a tortoise. Over the years of their journey through life, they have learned to accommodate their differences in energy.

Connie always insists on the "five o'clock cocktail hour" before dinner that balances Ted's tendency to burn himself out. At 5:00 p.m., he stops whatever project he is involved in—and he always is—to sit with her for an hour and debrief the day over a glass of wine or a cup of tea. You can visibly observe him power down his systems and relax into her company, dinner, and the evening together. Ted has the internal security to allow himself to be balanced and influenced by Connie, to his personal benefit and a harmonious relationship.

Now that they are both retired, it is not unusual for Ted to have tended to the garden and put in a couple of sets of tennis before Connie rolls out of bed. They both face serious health issues at this point. Their previous roles have evaporated in the wake of a series of surgeries they have each undergone. During recovery, whatever tasks need to be accomplished are done by whoever is best able to do it. Their relationship is a dance; life is a dance.

The Starks' evening reconnecting ritual was established early in their marriage when they had young children. The children were taught to respect their parents' hour alone, and interruptions were not tolerated. The hour before dinner was the children's time to play quietly and settle into the evening routine. "Okay, kids, it's quiet time now; you can read or play a game, but you have to be quiet and let Mommy and Daddy talk."

MODELING SELF-CARE

Most couples with young children buy into the notion that it is impossible to carve out quality time together with youngsters in the home. When children are permitted to dictate the emotional climate and household schedule, chaos is the result. Children need parents who take care of themselves and their relationship. If parents can't manage to take care of themselves and their relationship, how can the children trust them?

Children are not developmentally equipped to be in charge, but it is their job to try. When they succeed, they feel insecure and do not learn respect for authority. Where else will they learn the importance of self-care in marriage? A child's classroom is the family of origin.

Children learn that a contented and successful life includes obeying the rules of society that safeguard our cherished traditions, systems and freedoms. They need to understand what is expected of them and be held to firm but fair boundaries in order to feel secure. Children do not have the emotional development or life experience to be in charge and they sense it.

When expectations are clear and begun early, children learn how to read situations and develop a repertoire of appropriate behaviors to navigate within them.

In every setting, there are rules to be observed in order to fit in and find acceptance and belonging. Parents who allow children to run the household without enforced rules, appropriate behavior, and defined boundaries do not adequately prepare children for school or life. Shirking this parenting responsibility is a type of abuse that sets children up for rejection and failure outside the family.

Resisting, testing boundaries, and rebelling against parental authority is a necessary and predictable part of a child's development. Parents can consider this a significant opportunity to teach a reality of life: there will always be the needs of others to consider, authorities who tell you what to do, and rules to be obeyed.

CHALLENGES

Keeping your intimate relationship healthy is an investment in the future. In the throes of child-bearing years, and in juggling the myriad demands of work, housekeeping, childcare, relationship and couple time, it is impossible to imagine a time when there will be only two of you. Parenthood is a stage—only twenty years of a lifetime. With today's extended longevity and vigor, seniors want to remain employed and engaged with life.

The decline in economic security has also signaled the end of an era where the empty nest ushered in the so-called "golden years." It is largely a phenomenon of the past. Today, the years after launching the children are the beginning of a new life and exciting opportunities as individuals and as a couple.

Neglecting self-care and your individual interests because of the children is not the same as making family a priority. Seeing the two as mutually exclusive is a false dilemma, modeling the wrong values. Teaching children effective ways of dealing with authority, advocating for themselves, respecting differences, and handling conflict are needed skills that begin in the home.

Keep in mind that the marital relationship and the vitality of the individual partners come first. Secondly, partners working together find solutions fair to everyone. A lush, loving, lively marriage is the greatest gift to your children.

What are the practical, financial, and emotional challenges a couple faces in carving out time for individual activities and leisure time? Child-care arrangements, children's activities, discretionary money, extended family obligations, and health concerns are a few of the roadblocks. The emotional considerations we touched on previously are more subtle but can be equally significant challenges.

RESOLUTIONS

When you have young children, an avid bicyclist may not be able to join his club on frequent weekend cycling excursions. But other ways can be found to stay fit and participate on a weekend once or twice a year. Including one child in a parent's favorite activity is a wonderful tradition to start.

Alone time with a parent in a shared passion is a special treat for parent and child. Singling out a child for quality time alone with a parent allows the two of you to get to know each other on an entirely different level. These precious times pay off down the line when adolescent ambivalence and rebellion sets in. A fishing or hiking enthusiast might share weekend camping trips with a child. Many activities are amenable to creative adjustments and should begin at an early age.

It is not fair for a partner to take off for the day or weekend alone on a regular basis and ask the spouse to pick up the slack. If both partners are employed outside the home, many things need to be done on the weekend such as laundry, shopping, children's athletic events, etc. The fairness and equality rule is as important in this agreement as in any other. Remember, no one wins unless everyone wins.

EXERCISES

Make a "Wish List" of things that each of you would love to do in your leisure time. These might be activities you engaged in before or things you would like to learn or resume. Go over your lists together:

1. What do you both enjoy that you could engage in together?

2. What can do with one of your children?

3. What can you do as a family?

4. What are strictly solo activities?

5. Circle those realistic activities that you would like to fit into your schedule.

6. Prioritize.

7. Choose several activities as possibilities to implement.

Discussion

What activities of you or your partner are too time-and-money intensive to pursue at this time in your life and must be postponed?

OUR AGREEMENT ON LEISURE TIME

EXTENDED FAMILY & OTHER SIGNIFICANT RELATIONSHIPS

Part IV: Extended Family & Other Significant Relationships

PROLOGUE

There is no way around the fact that humans are social beings. It's all about relationships from beginning to end. When your relationships are healthy and satisfying…life is great. When your relationships are troubled…life sucks. Not exactly elegant language, but it expresses what you feel.

In the beginning of life, your physical and emotional survival depends on someone falling in love with you and taking care of you. Gazing into your beloved mother's face while receiving nourishment from the breast, your infant self feels no separation between mother and you…it's absolute bliss! It's a feeling you spend your life trying to replicate with a beloved other than mother.

Even if you were one of the lucky few who had the ideal experience as an infant, the adult relationship with your family of origin is an emotional quagmire. The whole work of becoming a differentiated adult requires heart-wrenching disengagement from the caretakers your childhood emotional and physical survival was dependent upon. As if that were not complicated enough, you have to come to an acceptance that it's normal to have dependency needs and still be a healthy adult.

Driven to find a beloved life partner, when you finally do, you have just doubled the whole family of origin equation. Remember the crowded bed book cover described earlier, the young couple with a set of parents lying on either side? Now recall that the latest brain research indicates that the differentiation process can't be completed until age 35-45, and you begin to understand that life is not about arrival… it's about the journey! And the only aspect of the journey that ultimately matters is measured in the quality of your relationships.

The following two chapters go in depth into the satellite relationships surrounding your partnership with your beloved and how to handle the myriad issues that arise. Apply the Rules and Guidelines you learned in this book to all your relationships.

> *"Life is not a problem to be solved*
> *But a mystery to be embraced."* [1]

Embrace the mystery! Live gracefully…in love and laughter, harmony and accord!

OUR GOALS FOR EXTENDED FAMILY &
OTHER SIGNIFICANT RELATIONSHIPS

Secret #11

PARENTING, STEP-PARENTING & GRAND-PARENTING

Perhaps you have read this far, but you are not yet parents, never had children, or your children are grown and gone. Even so, don't skip this chapter. You will discover a great deal more about how you came to be who you are from an entirely new and different perspective. Learning about parenting pitfalls and healthy practices may contribute to your understanding of the subconscious scripts and messages you internalized as a child and which continue silently to sabotage your best intentions and life goals.

THE LEGACY OF CHILDHOOD

Difficulties in adult relationships stem from the reality that, as children, both you and your partner were held hostage to your upbringing and it is a lingering legacy. As a child, you may have had an instinctive awareness that something was wrong and there must be a better way, but you didn't have the means to access and evaluate other options.

Childhood experience expands with the advent of school, and children begin to gather information from influences outside the family of origin. Life includes other children and visits to homes with different manners, values, and traditions. Classroom and playground rules articulate standards of conduct and sportsmanship. The world opens to you and you gather and internalize a storehouse of information about navigating the universe outside your family.

In adolescence, you incorporate the information you have assimilated into the foundation of your personal identity. A large part of that identity is influenced by what you have garnered about what it means to be a man or a woman, by observation and experience, but without the developmental maturity to interpret or evaluate them by any objective standard of reality. In addition, you were encumbered by the overwhelming emotions, drives, and roles of adolescence. At least a dozen years before completing the developmental tasks and barely out of adolescence, more than likely, you fell in love and married.

BACKGROUND TO PARENTING

An adolescent is in a rush to leave childhood with its dependence and helplessness behind…to forget what it is like to be a child. On becoming a parent, it is important to reclaim your experience. It is your responsibility to revise history from an adult perspective in order to prevent passing along to your children the behaviors and events that wounded you as a child. Have you ever noticed and wondered at the number of times in Jesus' brief ministry he drew attention to children?

At that time the disciples came to Jesus and asked, 'Who is the greatest in the kingdom of heaven?' He called a child, whom he put among them, and said, 'Truly I tell you, unless you change and become like children, you will never enter the kingdom of heaven. Whoever becomes humble like this child is the greatest in the kingdom of heaven. Whoever welcomes one such child in my name welcomes me.
(Matthew 18:1-5)

On those occasions, Jesus was speaking to adults. Why would he repeatedly refer to children when addressing adults? For our purposes, assume the prophet Isaiah's words, *"and a child shall lead them"* (Isaiah 11:6) and Jesus' words *"Let the children come unto me..."* (Matthew 19:14; Luke 18:16) were not meaningless platitudes, but directives of incredible wisdom.

'If any of you put a stumbling-block before one of these little ones who believe in me, it would be better for you if a great millstone were fastened around your neck and you were drowned in the depth of the sea. Woe to the world because of stumbling-blocks! Occasions for stumbling are bound to come, but woe to the one by whom the stumbling-block comes!
(Matthew 18:6-7)

Strong words! What are the stumbling-blocks you as a parent put in the way of your children's security and happiness? What are the stumbling-blocks that betray your children's faith and trust? What are the stumbling-blocks that interfere with your child's optimal emotional development? What are the stumbling-blocks that destroy your children's innocence? What are the "stumbling-blocks" that undermine healthy future relationships for your children?

Avoiding the creation of stumbling-blocks sounds like a tall order for parents…an unattainable goal. But stumbling-blocks are choices and within your power to control. Stumbling-blocks come from a Closed Heart place and you can choose an Open Heart at each opportunity until it becomes your default.

When you are in conflict with your spouse over parenting, your children are caught in the middle. They feel responsible and it places them in a double-bind that wounds them.

> *'Take care that you do not despise [ignore, hurt, or neglect] one of these little ones; for, I tell you, in heaven their angels continually see the face of my Father in heaven.…So it is not the will of your Father in heaven that one of these little ones be lost.'* (Matthew 18: 10, 14)

When Jesus speaks of "despise":

> Despise: to regard with contempt, distaste, disgust, or disdain; scorn; loathe.

Isn't he talking about disregarding the emotional wounds your words and actions inflict when children are the targets of or witnesses to hateful words or actions? Isn't he talking about the legacy of pain and trust issues caused by divorce?

Whatever your faith, Jesus' words are a commentary on the awesome responsibility of parenting. When we study the words and actions of Jesus' life as a man, when we imagine that he was modeling how to live in communion with others, we notice that everything he said and did was significant. In this regard, notice he always acted from an Open Heart, and assume his repeated reference to learning from children was intentional. Perhaps it would be simpler to consider that the innocence, trust, openness, and love with which young children approach life is the secret to happiness and success in life.

Loving and protecting children is a commonly accepted responsibility of caring parents, but inviting their wisdom and input, learning from them, being led by them is not. As always, we are asked to take a step beyond, to stretch ourselves, to reach outside default beliefs and behaviors.

WHEN PARENTS CAN'T AGREE

Parenting conflicts are one of the top four issues challenging couples. A fundamental reason exists for parenting being in the top four; it is the primary battleground in which the struggle previously defined as "whose dysfunctional family of origin is going to prevail" is most pernicious.

Both partners come into marriage with an internal model for raising children based on the way their parents raised them. Even when you are aware of the ways your parents failed, you tend to default to the embedded script…until you intentionally replace them with parenting guidelines of your own.

An undifferentiated partner still accepts that the family of origin reflects on his or her individual identity as a person. As long as the "my family is me" (fusion) belief prevails, your ability objectively to consider family-of-origin dysfunctions is hampered. The issues are buried until triggered when you become a parent. An endless series of unresolved issues may rise to the surface at any time and create tension and conflict between parents.

In the absence of reflection, history often repeats itself, and parents are vulnerable to passing on to their children unhealthy patterns from the past. Understanding our lives can free us from the otherwise almost predictable situation in which we recreate the damage to our children that was done to us. By making sense of our lives we can deepen a capacity for self-understanding and bring coherence to our emotional experience, our views of the world, and our interactions with our children.[1]

Difficulties can show up at any age in your child's life. The important thing for you as a parent and spouse to keep in mind is that some unattended childhood wound has been tapped. The danger is in being blindsided and striking out at your spouse or child. Your responsibility is to own your feelings and regulate your response.

The best course—as always—is to look inward to find the woundedness at the source of your feelings. First, we will take a look at predictable challenges of specific benchmark ages. At the end of this chapter, you will find exercises to help you work through these issues and restore effective communication.

THE BIRTH OF A CHILD

It appears to be in both mothers and fathers' natures, not just in mothers, to respond to parenting with hormonal changes. A new mother's maternal instincts and a powerful hormone, oxytocin, kick in and her total focus is on baby, as it is meant to be.

The initial month or so of a newborn's life ideally is an intensive bonding and adjustment period between mother and baby. The first few weeks are critical for secure attachment in the rapidly developing emotional center of the brain. The hippocampus in the brain's core runs the limbic system upon which an entire lifetime of positive expectations and self-concept are laid down.

> *Parent-child relationships offer a very important part of the early experience that directly shapes a child's emerging personality. Emotional intelligence, self-esteem, cognitive abilities and social skills are built on the early attachment relationship.*[2]

Surprising new research shows that hormonal changes also take place in men who take an active role in parenting.

> *Testosterone, that most male of hormones, takes a dive after a man becomes a parent. And the more he is involved in caring for his children—changing diapers, jiggling the boy or girl on his knee, reading "Goodnight Moon" for the umpteenth time—the lower his testosterone drops.*

> *Experts say the research has implications for understanding the biology of fatherhood, hormone roles in men and even health issues like prostate cancer.*[3]

A self-referencing husband/father is available to support the luminous falling-in-love period, and protect the invisible bubble surrounding mother and infant. He feels deeply involved by caring for his infant's bathing and diapering needs, comforting a cranky baby, and making sure Mom gets sufficient rest. He feels secure in his role and filled up with selfless love and gratitude for the blessing of this precious new family.

It is not unusual for new fathers to feel displaced by a first offspring. If you, as a father, have ever felt this way, rather than beating yourself up, take it as a sign that you have some unfinished business in differentiation. Perhaps unresolved sibling rivalry exists in your family of origin. Don't allow the past to poison the present and future.

Science continues to validate the wisdom of ancient spiritual traditions regarding the way we humans are designed. If you have as a goal to become active partners in parenting, you are cooperating with your natures rather than being at war with them. This mindset is also consistent with the following promise in the Scriptures:

> *Again, truly I tell you, if two of you agree on earth about anything you ask, it will be done for you by my Father in heaven. For where two or three are gathered in my name, I am there among them.* (Matthew 18: 19-20)

This passage is rarely invoked in the context of the family… but when it is, this assurance alone might mitigate most conflict. Surely, two parents seeking Divine blessing on their marriage and their children fall within the bounds of this promise.

ROOTS OF CONFLICT

Even when you are aware of the flaws in your parents' methods, on becoming a parent yourself, you may feel defensive of your defaults if you have not staked a claim to your own parenting strategy.

Inevitably, your spouse has a different history, a different script, and a different perspective on the correct way to parent. If the two of you have not mutually agreed upon your own brand of parenting, butting heads over child-rearing practices is almost guaranteed. During conflict, your spouse may be cast as the enemy rather than the partner. Lack of a parenting plan leads to crazy-making for the couple and the children, who feel guilty for causing conflict.

As partners, you must examine and learn from mistakes of the past, preserve the traditions and practices that meet your values and objectives, refine and re-define your parenting goals as you grow and learn, and attune and attend to your children's individual needs and temperaments.

In order to achieve objectivity for this task, parents have to embark on the difficult work of breaking the fusion—and confusion—from their families of origin, and differentiate themselves from them. The goal is to cultivate awareness and objectivity—not as simple as it sounds.

THEN VS. NOW

In previous generations, it was a popular parenting notion that parents present a "united front" to their children. The operative word is front—actually pretense or even deception is a more accurate definition of the term front. The implication is that any disagreements between parents should be concealed from the children. This belief may be a misinterpretation of the "one flesh" command.

Actually, children fare better with the reality that parents have disagreements. Otherwise, they blame themselves and learn to be deceitful and conceal the truth. For one thing, children are not fooled. They pick up on hidden emotional disturbances; they are merely distressed about the causes, and likely to blame themselves.

A united front neither models differences between people who love each other, nor instills a process for negotiation. Unfortunately, the "united front" principle persists in some contexts, especially among Christian couples, even though the principle has been discredited.

PARTNERS IN PARENTING

This is a chapter on parenting in a book on partnering. It is not meant to be a book on parenting. However, if parenting is one of the four top areas of conflict in a marriage, it cannot be overlooked in a book dedicated to effective communication, harmony, and accord in marriage. With that in mind, let's spend a little time with some ideas for parenting that you may have never considered.

Thinking ahead to the role-modeling that parents present to their children requires two emotionally mature people taking responsibility for their individual and joint behavior. When undifferentiated people find themselves in a parenting role, they attempt either to reverse the parenting model they experienced or to emulate it.

Undifferentiated and immature people are likely to manipulate their partner and children for their own personal needs, with little awareness of the potential damage. All these consequences result in personality traits and attitudes that undermine social acceptance and successful relationships. These resulting problems are not emphasized in current parenting culture.

Prevailing parenting practices in our culture may actually promote fusion rather than differentiation. If you are able to agree on the wisdom of the following principles for child-rearing, perhaps it will turn things around and get you on the same parenting wave-length.

POPULAR MISCONCEPTIONS

Parents have taken to heart the message that it is important to build self-esteem in our children so they come into adulthood having confidence in their abilities to succeed. Today's parents are lavish in their praise; "Good job," "I am so proud of you," and "You were amazing," are often voiced and well-intentioned comments.

Such comments are warranted until the age of two. Toddlers thrive on praise and encouragement. By age three, however, the benefits begin to reverse. Parents need to shift gradually and give recognition for effort, persistence, contribution, and sharing. Kids figure out the difference between ritual praise and earned praise very early.

The definition of success in this context is generally measured in status and the material trappings of accomplishment, the hallmark of a competitive culture. Children learn to measure love and approval in terms of getting what they want, whether it is attention, food, or stuff. They want what they see advertised on TV, what their siblings have, and what their friends have. They want what they want when they want it, and parents give into them because it is the path of least resistance. Parents give in because children play on their feelings of inadequacy and guilt.

Children are masters at pushing buttons to get what they want. When children win at the manipulation game, they lose. They fight to be in charge, but if they succeed, they are insecure. Indulgent parenting is lazy parenting. Praise-centric parenting is indulgent and irresponsible.

Indulged children are not equipped for a world outside the home that has little interest in what they want. Society judges them by their character, their ability to relate well with others, and their achievements. Conscientious parenting should be more concerned with teaching values and behaviors that build character and lead to successful relationships rather than material success.

Natural gifts are an accident of birth, such as beauty, music, art, intelligence, athletics, etc. These are to be acknowledged and nurtured, but the use of praise is meant to reinforce how they develop and use their gifts—for their effort, overcoming difficulties, commitment, and teamwork, all qualities that build character, but do not instill a sense of superiority over others.

It is more important to praise children for honorable character and success measured by improvement in their own personal best rather than measured against the achievement of others. Support behaviors that help children gain acceptance from others due to who they are, as opposed to what they accomplish. Use praise as a means to emphasize behaviors you admire in your own friends, such as:

- Working things out for themselves

- Empathy and compassion toward others

- Persistence and effort

- Achievement earned from effort

- Coming through a difficult time

- Generosity and unselfishness

- Eagerness to help

- A positive attitude even when thwarted

- Grace under pressure

Undeserved praise leads to a variety of adverse consequences, one of which is promoting the need for approval from others rather than differentiation. Other consequences include a sense of entitlement, dependence on others for validation, and unwillingness to accept responsibility for their thoughts, feelings, and behavior.

Unearned praise may result in a false sense of superiority that has recently been implicated in the rise of bullying behavior. The need to constantly feed an oversized ego without a solid core self-concept can lead to perpetual contempt for others.

STEP-PARENTING

The issues of step-parenting are loaded and complex. Rarely does divorce solve the problems a couple hopes divorce will resolve, so the unfinished business of the marriage gets played out in the arena of parenting. The first spouse to remarry generally takes the most heat. There may be envy, jealousy, competition, anger, blame, guilt, and regret to confront in either or both of the divorced spouses.

Children are the final battleground of a failed marriage. Unfortunately, very few divorcing couples work through the grief, disappointment, and anger together. They do it through the courts, thereby increasing the animosity. Then the former partners rush to replace the lost love. At least half of today's couples deal with the complexity of single parenting or blended families.

Parenting mistakes in the first marriage are complicated by the divorce's unfinished business. Adding to the complications are differences in a new partner's parenting beliefs and stepchildren who are scarred, scared, and angry. All of the above issues apply with the added challenges of parenting practices that differ between two parents and two households. Add to these obstacles the interference of previous spouses and multiple sets of grandparents.

Most couples benefit from a neutral outside party to navigate these turbulent waters and protect the innocence and security of all the children involved. Certain therapists specialize in treating children whose parents are divorcing and families who are blending. Coming to a mutual agreement about how to handle parenting and step-parenting issues in your household is the first step.

GRAND-PARENTING

Grand-parenting truly is a minefield! All the guilt, regrets, and insecurities of all the people involved crowd the field. New parents are flooded with unexpected feelings of love, vulnerability, protectiveness, responsibility, fear, and self-doubt. Once again, the ultimate cost of avoiding the work of becoming emotionally mature is paid by the youngest and most vulnerable of the generations…and the dysfunction beat goes on.

Grandparents grasp at the opportunity for a second chance to get it right, or prove they were right…in either case it is an approach with potentially devastating consequences. The new parents are inundated with advice that makes them feel even more overwhelmed, inadequate, and perhaps even angry. The grandparents are disappointed and confused that their gifts born of wisdom and painful experience are reject-ed. Misunderstanding and tension grow between the genera-tions, and everyone feels at a loss to halt the downward slide.

Healthy, supportive grand-parenting is built on the same foundation as all healthy relationships—differentiation. Another term synonymous with differentiation is self-refer-enced, as opposed to other-referenced. Again, we're talking about learning to find positive feelings about yourself within yourself. For grandparents, it means respecting the new par-ents' right to muddle through on their own, find their own way, make their own mistakes, and trust that what you gave them is enough.

EXERCISES & DISCUSSION

Needs of the Children

- Define parenting outcomes in general and for each child in the home.

- Describe in detail what kind of person each child will become.

- Consider what makes each child unique:

  - What are each child's special talents and abilities?

  - What are the qualities you most admire in each child?

  - What kind of discipline does each child respond to? (One size does NOT fit all!)

  - What type of approval does each child need?

For Parents

1. Establish mutual standards, values, and boundaries for this household.

2. How will you handle parenting differences?

3. Decide on who has final authority over the children whom each spouse brings to the marriage.

4. Determine what authority each spouse has over step-children.

5. Discuss what messages are okay to convey regarding the children's absent parent.

6. Who has final authority in handling decisions: either by biological parent or gender of the child and the parent?

7. List at least three good ways your parents supported you that you would like to pass along to your children.

8. What kind of relationship do you want with your children when they are adults?

9. What do you wish your parents had done or not done in parenting you?

For Grandparents

1. What kind of parenting advice and/or behaviors were you willing to accept from your parents when you were new parents?

2. What drove you crazy?

3. What would you have liked to say to them?

For Stepparents

1. If your parents divorced, remember what it was like for you. What did you need from your parents at the time? How can the memory guide your own step-parenting practices?

2. If your parent(s) remarried, what did you need from your stepparent(s)?

3. What is the advice you would give couples entering into a second marriage with children in the home?

4. Processing Negative Feelings Toward a Child or Step-child

5. Did something significant or traumatic happen to you when you were the child's age?

6. What feelings come up when you remember that event?

7. Trace back to times when you felt this way as an adult.

8. How did your parents relate to you when you were your child's age?

9. Do the troubling feelings come up with just one of your children or all of them?

Partners Without Children

1. So you hung in there through this chapter! To make the most of it, complete the exercises above that may be relevant to you as well as the following:

2. What new thought did you discover about how you were parented?

3. If your parents were divorced, what distressing memories came up for you?

4. If you had a stepparent, how did you feel about it at the time? Now?

5. How has the experience affected you as a partner? Your marriage?

6. If you have grown children, do you realize some mistakes you made?

7. What do you wish you could do over? (Be specific.)

8. How could you talk about your mistakes with your grown child to make amends?

9. How will the principles discussed in this chapter influence your parenting if or when you become parents?

OUR AGREEMENT FOR PARENTING, STEP-PARENTING & GRAND-PARENTING

Secret #12

EXTENDED FAMILY, FRIENDS, EXES & IN-LAWS

You came into marriage with a history of relationships with people who are meaningful to you. Among them are parents, extended family, friends, in-laws, and business associates. If you are divorced, you also have exes and ex in-laws. If you have children from a prior marriage, there are your exes' parents and grandparents who also have a stake in your life!

Your spouse has the same ensemble on his or her side of the equation. Is there any way for this to be less than complex? Is it any wonder that all these relationships are often a hotbed of conflict for couples?

Refer back to previous discussions regarding fusion vs. intimacy. Couples who are still confused about the difference between fusion and intimacy may be threatened by a partner's loyalty to family of origin and single friends. The conflicts that arise are literally fighting in the dark because the underlying issues are so complex and obscure.

Couples feel increasingly angry and helpless when they don't really understand what they are fighting about. So much misunderstanding and damage can result while the couple struggles to make sense of what is happening to them. This area is an emotionally loaded one for couples who are not adequately differentiated.

Especially early in marriage, young individuals lack the maturity and awareness of the ways in which internalized, inherited scripts dictate the roles and rules under which they operate. Until becoming self-referenced, you continue to hold the conviction that all of these people have a claim on you. And they do.

It becomes a problem in your relationship when you allow others to define what their claim is on your life. Setting the boundaries is up to you. Recall one of the original Rules and Guidelines...others are not allowed to be comfortable at your expense.

ESTABLISHING PRIORITIES AND BOUNDARIES

The following section has been introduced before, but it will be reiterated in this section because it has a slightly different and significant twist. In particular, parents, friends, and exes are reluctant to surrender their previous position of significance in your life.

This zone is potentially hazardous in a young marriage, and if not navigated with awareness and intention, can damage the trust you are trying to foster. You may inadvertently cast your spouse as an interloper rather than a partner, or alienate others who matter to you.

Revisit the cautionary message in Scripture commanding a shift in alliance when two partners commit to one another. In this chapter, it has a different implication and bears repeating.

> *"For this **reason** a man will leave his father and mother and be united to his wife, and they will become one flesh."* (Genesis 2:24)

This teaching is so vital that it shows up immediately after God's creation of man and woman. It appears prior to sex, and refers to a father and mother before either even existed! It is repeated again by Christ in the Gospels. It appears twice, in Matthew and in Mark. The first half of the two-part command instructs you about where your allegiance lies once you marry, and there don't seem to be any exceptions to the rule.

In the second half of the verse, obviously His words regarding **uniting** and **becoming one flesh** do not refer only to sex, as it is generally interpreted. Sexual union had not yet entered the picture. He was talking about what is required to form a union that becomes **one flesh**. If "one flesh" doesn't refer to those moments of physical union in sex, what does it mean the rest of the time?

For the answer, we need to back up and consider the entire context of this verse. The verse refers to a **"reason"** that gives rise to the command that follows. What is that **"reason"**?

> *The LORD God said, "It is not good for the man to be alone. I will make a helper suitable for him."* (Genesis 2:18)

The King James version uses the word "helpmeet," which is perhaps a clearer description of the intended relationship. Pay attention to the order and the context. God had just created the Garden of Eden, shown Adam around, and charged him with the responsibility of caring for it. It was then that He noted it was "not good for the man to be alone."

> *Now the LORD God had formed out of the ground all the beasts of the field and all the birds of the air. He brought them to the man to see what he would name them; and whatever the man called each living creature, that was its name. So the man gave names to all the livestock, the birds of the air and all the beasts of the field.* ***But for Adam no suitable helper was found.***
> (Genesis 2:19-20)

Is it a stretch to interpret that God intended the man and his wife to be partners in tending to all that He had created? Is it possible that when God mused that it was not good for man to be alone, he meant that the nature of woman and her different outlook was needed in all spheres of the running of the planet?

Traditionally, the verse has been interpreted strictly in terms of relationship. I think it means that the feminine perspective provides a balance. Her hormones, her ability to create and nurture life, her fiercely protective nature are all needed in life's operations.

What would your marriage look like if "becoming one flesh" were interpreted to mean that you are commanded to confront anything that comes between husband and wife as the "thief in the night"…the enemy, the intruder into a sacred space? Even if the "intruder" is someone extremely important to you?

It is important to have an individual life of your own. It is important to nurture the relationships that are meaningful to you. It is important to be responsive to the people in your life whom you care about. But how do you fit it all in and stay true to conflicting commitments?

It is not something you can figure out unilaterally; this matter requires negotiation and mutual agreement. First, we'll consider each category in depth to provide a basis for your discussion. All of the following applies to each spouse; however, the family history and relationships may be very different for each of you.

SHIFTING LOYALTIES

It takes time for individuals to process the shift of loyalties from their family of origin to their beloved. It may seem that the individual raised in a close, nurturing family would find the separation more difficult, but that is not generally the case. Counter-intuitively, the transition is even more difficult for individuals who did not get nurturing and support from their family. They tend either to idealize their parents or deny that the deficits had any impact on them.

In any case, under-nurtured children of any age are liable to be over-sensitive to criticism directed at their family and defend it as if their life depended on it. Parents who are unaware or selfish may inadvertently fuel the conflict by asking their grown child to validate their weak self-esteem, or assuage their guilt by proving their loyalty in all sorts of convoluted ways.

A CHILD'S PERSPECTIVE

Your most complex relationship in your life is the one with your parents; your first relationship began with them and that relationship never ends. You have been deeply exploring your family of origin as it impacts your relationship and you are growing in understanding and objectivity. This knowledge provides insight into yourself and your way of being in a relationship.

This chapter is about how you relate to parents as an adult with a spouse and a family of your own. What is an appropriate relationship between your parents and you as a grown child with a family of your own? What demands are acceptable for your parents to make on you? Where do your primary loyalties lie?

Most people will have some of these issues, but hopefully not all. Some general principles can offer guidance through the process. If you have feelings about your parents that plague you, such as uncertainty, confusion, obligation, guilt, or shame, it is likely a sign of unfinished business and/or incomplete differentiation.

Most couples unconsciously choose to get into conflict with each other over parents, rather than doing the work of sorting things out with their parents. You may not see avoidance as the basis of the parent issue, but generally it is.

A PARENT'S PERSPECTIVE

Whenever I see a celebrity interview, some variation of the inevitable question is asked, "With all your success, what achievement are you most proud of?" Without exception, the answer has been, "My children!"

All caring parents feel the burden of responsibility for the well-being of their children. Conscientious parents think about the future and try to prepare their children to face life. The problem is that undifferentiated parents are ill-equipped to encourage differentiation in their children. Actually, parents ask their children—in overt or covert ways—to validate them.

From your parents' point of view, they are still seeking acknowledgment and acceptance. Parents need to feel as important as they did when you were young and dependent. They need to be reassured that they were good parents, especially if they weren't. They want your love and approval as much as you needed theirs at one time. In fact, at this time in their lives, when there may be fewer sources of gratification from work, the need for meaningful connection and validation from you can be more important than ever before.

If your struggle for individuation didn't begin during the infamous "adolescent rebellion," engaging your parents at this late stage is likely to meet with shock and resistance. The greater your parents' emotional dependency—lack of differentiation—the greater their defensiveness. They may feel betrayed by your belated impulse to become a self-referencing person.

The balance of power shifts when children are grown. Parents usually do not consider this future change when children are young and parents feel totally in control. Parents treat their young children as if they will never have to be accountable for their parenting choices and behavior.

Struggling to establish an appropriate relationship that is healthy for you and your nuclear family is a moment of truth for both you and your parents.

ADULT CHILD'S PERSPECTIVE

An adolescents' push for independence will often counter the beliefs of their parents, at least for a time. An adolescent reaction against authority is developmental opposition, not authentic differentiation. It is simply a continuation of the individuation process beginning at age two and going in spurts and starts throughout childhood.

If you haven't been intentionally committed to the process of differentiation before now, you are not alone. You and your partner are making a commitment to change the course of the future from the dysfunctional patterns of the past. Designing a resilient and viable future for your marriage and your family requires getting intentional about doing the work of differentiation.

THE ABUSIVE FAMILY

Even if you had good parents, they made mistakes that hurt you. They are often unaware of the pain they caused or the ways they undermined your faith in yourself. But not all parents were well-intentioned. If you were subjected to violence, addiction, abuse, and neglect in childhood, you are justified in feeling blame, anger, and resentment. Acknowledging the dysfunction in your family of origin and making a conscious decision to be different from your family members is not the same as differentiation.

In fact, the lack of healthy role models muddles the process of differentiation. It is further complicated if the abusive or addicted parents have since cleaned up their acts and consider the bad times as in the past. When they see you functioning as an effective, competent adult, they expect to be treated as if they have been good parents all along, but you are still seething. Consider seeking professional help or a Twelve-Step group for survivors to support you in getting past this hurdle.

THE WAY FORWARD

So how do you deal appropriately with the multi-faceted parent situation? If your parents divorced and remarried, you have two sets of parents to deal with. If your spouse comes from a broken family too, four sets of parents are in your life. If your biological parents have unfinished business resulting in unresolved resentment and animosity, there is likely a confusion of emotional debris in the relational field.

Your instincts are to protect your nuclear family from this fallout, but you may not know how to do that without shutting out your parents and inadvertently escalating the emotional intensity.

Strike a chord? Never fear...the way out is your old friend: self-referencing/differentiation! Sound like a broken record? This is the final chapter of the book, so if you haven't learned to spell differentiation by now, try out this spelling...FREE-DOM!

The only way to cut the ties that bind is differentiation. A hallmark of a self-referenced person's relationships is the ability to set boundaries in a powerful and caring way, not a reactive or antagonistic one.

If you have unresolved issues—like the ones listed above—standing in the way of forgiving the past, you need to address them as an adult, not as a hurt, helpless child or an acting-out adolescent. No matter how conscientious you are as a parent, you too will hurt and disappoint your children. Put yourself in your parents' shoes. How can your children approach you in a way you can hear them? This shift in perspective shows you a way forward with your parents and with your own children.

The balance of power has changed, so your parents now need what you needed as a child—clear guidelines within which to function with assurance that they will have your approval and respect. You will not be able to establish clear boundaries if the emotional waters between you and your parents remain muddy.

The first step is to continue the internal work of clearing the field, becoming self-referenced. Second, to continue the process of building a stable and satisfying marriage, including clear values and boundaries.

Parents, deserving or undeserving, are not exempt from the rules and guidelines laid out at the very beginning of Dynamic Marriage. Those rules and guidelines apply to *all* your relationships.

FRIENDS

Friends you had prior to marriage can be a cause of dissension, particularly if they are still single and expect to conduct the relationship as it was before you married. Even if they are in a relationship, your friends may not have the same values and priorities for marriage as you.

When close friends compete for a spouse's time and attention, it is a no-win situation for everyone. A spouse who draws attention to rivalry may be accused of controlling relationships and activities, and curtailing freedom.

It is not acceptable for anyone outside a marriage to behave in a way that requires a partner to choose between a spouse and another. Anyone includes parents, exes, in-laws, children, and friends. It is selfish—not loving—to put someone you care about in a loyalty bind. The story of David and Jane illustrates this situation.

> David and Larry were best friends and "drinking buddies" before they each married. Larry was an unacknowledged alcoholic; David was a social drinker. David's new wife noticed a troubling pattern when the two couples went on vacation together for a week about a year into their relationship.

> In the late afternoon, Larry broke out a case of beer and chided David into joining him, even though it was earlier than David usually drank. Larry continued to drink into the evening until bedtime. When David wanted to call it quits, Larry employed an adolescent tactic, questioning David's manhood to coerce David to continue drinking with him.

David's wife, Jane, was uncomfortable with the pattern, which was repeated each afternoon. She tried to talk with David about her concerns, but he felt in a loyalty bind and became defensive. Larry had been his best buddy long before he met Jane. He cared about his wife's opinion, but he couldn't accept that Larry had a drinking problem.

Jane had become good friends with Larry's wife Sammi, and saw that Larry was on a course that would eventually destroy his wife's respect. Larry and Sammi had two little children Jane cared about. She felt in an integrity bind.

Because of Jane's awareness and courage, David began to pay attention to the signs she pointed out. He finally had to accept the reality that Larry did indeed have a problem that could cost him his family.

Jane and he agreed on a strategy for David to resist Larry's attempts to seduce David into drinking with him. When Larry and he were together, David claimed that he had made a decision not to drink when he was driving or around his family... "Off the sauce for a while" became his standard line to Larry.

David respected his wife's observation, and as a result, began to recognize the signs for himself. He was able to let go of his defensiveness and align his priorities. It is a typical strategy of addicts to coerce others to imbibe or get high so they can support their illusions that they don't drink or drug any more than normal people. In recovery circles, joining or provisioning someone who has a substance abuse issue is called "enabling."

The applicable guideline is: Whenever someone asks you to prove your love or loyalty backed-up by coercion or threat—no matter how disguised—it is not a legitimate or healthy interaction. Pay attention to your discomfort and voice it. You may need time to process and identify what is making you uncomfortable. The important thing is not to act until you feel clear.

EXES

The other parent of children from a previous marriage presents a considerably different dilemma. An ex does have a legitimate claim on his or her former spouse. But it is in nobody's best interest—especially not the children's—to allow or reward manipulation by ex-spouses by using the children.

Unresolved issues that you divorced to solve still have energy. A divorce rarely solves anything. Regret, anger, disillusion, and resentment don't simply die with the divorce decree. When new love enters your former spouse's life, it is disorienting, painful, and arouses old emotions you thought were buried.

Interference or competition from an ex-spouse is threatening to your new love, who is seeking to establish a secure position in your life together. If your new partner sees you can be manipulated into acting against your new loyalties by an ex-spouse, children, parents, or friends, he or she will lose respect, trust, and faith in your commitments, and your strength of character.

These qualities are easily lost and difficult to restore.

IN-LAWS

In-laws are frequently cast as bad guys in the marriage arena. Being an in-law is a high-wire act. If the parents have become aware of their "better late than never" mistakes as parents, they may be eager to make amends, which can look a lot like interference to young married couples.

If they have not grown in self-awareness, the parents may fight to retain their primary relationship with an adult child. This fight manifests as competing with the spouse, creating a loyalty bind for the adult child. In-laws may be defensive and seek validation of their parenting, which truly is interference.

Any or all these behaviors indicate that the in-laws feel insecure and uncertain about where they fit into their child's life in the new configuration, and they want to continue to feel important. If you have been working on your own growth in differentiation, you will be better prepared to deal with such in-laws and communicate your boundaries in a way that is firm and not rejecting.

If you need to cut your parents off to feel like an independent adult, it is a sign you are not yet fully differentiated. Please remember, differentiation is not a state you arrive at...it is a commitment to a lifetime journey of increasing awareness and openness to yourself and others.

It is not helpful to judge yourself against some arbitrary (and imaginary) standard of perfection. If you judge yourself, you will judge others. Instead, decide together what you need as a couple and establish clear boundaries for in-laws as well as parents.

The forgotten people in the drama of divorce are often the in-laws. Contrary to the cliché caricature of in-laws, caring parents often fall deeply in love with the person their child chooses as a life partner. They open their hearts and accept the spouse as one of their own.

When children divorce, and the son or daughter-in-law withdraws from their lives, they grieve. They suffer the loss of the loved person at family gatherings, celebrations, and holidays. When there are grandchildren, the parents of the non-custodial parent find their access to grandchildren severely curtailed and their influence as a significant presence in their lives evaporates. They grieve.

IN SUMMARY

Until the past half century, extended family provided a substantial context for grown children and their offspring. Grandparents represented support, maturity, wisdom, stability, and continuity to a new family. Young marriages were held by the elders. Children were born into a tribe. While that has changed in our highly-mobile culture, the emotional longing for belonging is alive in everyone, we all seek deep connections to a community.

Recall that we began this journey talking about the fact that loss and longing are inherent in the human experience. The longing for connection and belonging to a community are primary needs. Divorce is a consummate loss and further shatters the sense and security of belonging for everyone affected.

EXERCISES

Individual Preparation:

1. List the loss of important relationships that you have experienced in your life.

2. What do you need to do to get closure or resolution?

3. What longings in regards to relationships do you still have?

4. Are there significant people in your life whom you are in conflict with or harbor ill feelings toward?

5. What baggage from past relationships have you dragged into this relationship?

6. What people in your life are a burden rather than a blessing?

7. What stands in the way of letting go of resentment toward another?

8. How would the gift of forgiveness free you and gladden your heart?

9. What do you need to do to bring harmony and accord to those relationships?

Discussion:

Share your individual preparation and talk about each question with the objective of clearing the way for smooth sailing on your journey into the future.

OUR AGREEMENT ON EXTENDED FAMILY, FRIENDS, EXES & IN-LAWS

EPILOGUE

THE VOYAGE BEYOND

This is not an ending, but a beginning. The time spent mastering concepts and honing skills leads to rich relationships and joy in life. I attribute my love of the sea to my father. In my earliest memories, he took us to the beach and deep sea fishing. The last time I saw him alive, he had a beautiful poster showing a sailing vessel at anchor in a serene harbor at sunset. The message at the bottom said:

"a ship in a harbor is safe,
but that's not what ships are built for."

A ship is built for voyages across unknown and unpredictable seas…and all seas are unknown and unpredictable. Anything can happen at sea. Marriage is a voyage not a harbor. Intimate relationships are similar—unknown, unpredictable and anything can happen at any time. What are you built for? What gives meaning and purpose to your life? What gives grace and joy to your relationships?

Rick Warren's *The Purpose Driven Life* is the longest running best-selling book in history. Surely that is a testament to the hunger we humans have for a sense of purpose. We have an insatiable need to feel our lives have purpose and meaning. And relationships are key…to a Higher Power, ourselves and those we love.

"that's not what ships are built for."

It's pretty simple to understand what a ship is built for. But… what are you built for? Until you figure that out for yourself, or learn to live at peace with the mystery, you will continue to ask your relationships to fill the void—and they will always fail because it's not their responsibility. But they will get blamed for not meeting your expectations. And so will you, in your relationships that are unaware.

If you accept that relationships are responsible for your wounds, your fears, your longings, your losses and your self-concept—whatever it is—how do you plan to assure that they become healthy and happy? *Discovering a Dynamic Marriage* is the chart for your inaugural voyage, but ships… and relationships…are built for a lifetime of voyages.

Life's journey is made up of one voyage after another. Adolescence is a different trip from young parenthood, and empty nesting is an entirely different voyage than becoming elderly and once again dependent on others for survival… life coming full circle. It was always so…and always will be.

What is your next voyage? Bon Voyage!

Part Five

TOOLS & ILLUSTRATIONS: DIAGRAMS, WORKSHEETS & EXERCISES

Discovering
a Dynamic Marriage

EVENT

CHOICE

CLOSED HEART	OPEN HEART
WITHDRAW	**ENGAGE**
CASE-BUILD ▾ INTIMIDATE	UNDERSTAND ▪ APPRECIATE
DEFENSIVE ▪ STONEWALL	EMPATHIZE ▪ ENCOURAGE
CRITICIZE ▪ THREATEN	RESPOND ▪ VALIDATE
RESENT ▪ DISDAIN	RESPECT ▪ SUPPORT
BLAME ▪ RESIST	ACCEPT ▪ LISTEN
JUDGE ▪ REJECT	LAUGH ▪ LOVE
REJECT	LOVE
REJECT	LOVE
	LOVE

OPEN AND CLOSED HEART

The Open/Closed Heart is a theme running through *Discovering a Dynamic Marriage.* The diagram helps you identify specific emotional states and behavior associated with each stance. There is an important concept that needs clarification to use them appropriately. **Dynamic Marriage** deals with flawed and wounded human beings in flawed relationships. It is a given in the human realm.

There are common misconceptions about intimate relationships, and the Open Heart idea can feed into it and cause abuses. Popular thinking is that when you love someone you "give your heart" to the beloved. That is a dangerous thing to do. Who wants the responsibility? No one is so together that they are always in a place to be trusted with another's heart. When you love someone you invite him or her into your heart, but the safety of your heart is always your own responsibility.

When your partner is clearly not in a good place—triggered, hostile, out-of-sorts, overwhelmed, contentious, exhausted— you don't put your heart out there to be the target of abuse. Closing your heart to a beloved is rarely a good solution either. Recognizing the signs that your partner is not available does not put you in a Closed Heart place. On the contrary, allowing your partner to be emotionally out-of-commission for a time, without blame or judgment, is an Open Heart stance.

Blame and judgment are a result of putting your heart out there knowing your spouse is emotionally unavailable, and then blaming him or her for mistreating it. It is setting your spouse up to fail and prove that he or she can't be trusted.

That's old FOO stuff. It is convoluted, it is choosing to be right rather than related. Everyone is guilty of it at some point.

Another misuse of this exercise is to use it to manipulate. Accusing your partner of having a Closed Heart is an abuse of the intention and spirit of the exercise. It should never be used as a club. It is permissible to ask, but if you are wondering, it's usually safe to assume that your partner is closed, and postpone any important matters until he or she is emotionally available again.

In order to stay in an Open Heart place in the face of conflict and rough patches, you must consciously choose to take responsibility for your heart and protect it when necessary. It is a relief to know your partner will do the same thing when you go off the rails. Everybody gets to be less than perfect and still loved…everybody wins!

OPEN HEART RESPONSES

1. Examine your own customary loving responses and add any that may be missing for you.

2. Rank the responses according to the order they fade as tension or stress builds.

3. Recall an instance that you have felt this and try to understand where you learned it, when you resort to it, what you hope to accomplish, the impact on others, effectiveness, etc.

4. In terms of the goal of creating a "crucible" relationship that grows intimacy and individuals, does it deliver or damage?

5. What would you like to do more often?

6. How can your spouse/family support your growth?

Engage:

_____

_____

Understand:

_____

_____

Empathize:

_____

_____

Encourage:

_____

_____

Appreciate:

_____

_____

Respond:

_____

_____

Support:

_____

_____

Validate:

_____

_____

Respect:

_____

_____

Accept:

_____

_____

Listen:

_____

_____

Love:

_____

_____

CLOSED HEART RESPONSES

1. Examine your own default stress responses and add any that may be missing for you.

2. Rank the responses according to the order they show up as tension or stress builds.

3. Recall an instance that you have felt this and try to understand where you learned it, when you resort to it, what you hope to accomplish, its effectiveness, etc.

4. In terms of the goal of creating a "crucible" relationship that grows intimacy and individuals, does it deliver or damage?

5. What would you like to do instead?

6. How can your spouse/family support your growth?

Withdraw:

_____

_____

Intimidate:

_____

_____

Stonewalling:

_____

_____

Case-build:

_____

_____

Fault-finding:

_____

_____

Threaten:

_____

_____

Criticize:

_____

_____

Resent:

_____

_____

Defensive:

_____

_____

Resist:

_____

_____

Blame:

_____

_____

Judge:

_____

_____

Reject:

_____

_____

INVENTORY OF NEEDS

CONNECTION
acceptance
affection
belonging
cooperation
communication
closeness
community
companionship
compassion
consideration
consistency
empathy
inclusion
intimacy
love
mutuality
nurturing
respect/self-respect
understanding
warmth
sexual expression
touch

SUPPORT
safety
security
stability
trust
shelter
appreciation

HEALTH
oxygen
nutrition
movement
exercise
rest
sleep
water

HONESTY
authenticity
integrity
presence
trust

PLAY
joy
humor
laughter
games
holidays
celebration

PEACE
beauty
communion
ease
equality
harmony
inspiration
order

MEANING
awareness
challenge
clarity
consciousness
contribution
discovery
effectiveness
growth
learning
mourning
participation
purpose
stimulation
significance

AUTONOMY
choice
freedom
independence
personal space
spontaneity
competence
self-expression
creativity

SPIRITUAL
hope
celebration of life
faith
belief

INVENTORY OF FEELINGS

Feelings when your needs ARE satisfied

AFFECTIONATE
compassionate
friendly
loving
open hearted
sympathetic
tender
warm

CONFIDENT
empowered
open
proud
safe
secure

ENGAGED
absorbed
alert
curious
engrossed
enchanted
entranced
fascinated
interested
intrigued
involved
spellbound
stimulated

INSPIRED
amazed
awed
wonder

EXCITED
amazed
animated
ardent
aroused
astonished
dazzled
eager
energetic
enthusiastic
giddy
invigorated
lively
passionate
surprised
vibrant

EXHILARATED
blissful
ecstatic
elated
enthralled
exuberant
radiant
rapturous
thrilled

GRATEFUL
appreciative
moved
thankful
touched

HOPEFUL
expectant
encouraged
optimistic

JOYFUL
amused
delighted
glad
happy
jubilant
pleased
tickled

PEACEFUL
calm
clear headed
comfortable
centered
content
equananimous
fulfilled
mellow
quiet
relaxed
relieved
satisfied
serene
still
tranquil
trusting

REFRESHED
enlivened
rejuvenated
renewed
rested
restored
revived

INVENTORY OF FEELINGS

Feelings when your needs ARE NOT satisfied

AFRAID
apprehensive
dread
frightened
mistrustful
panicked
scared
suspicious
terrified
wary
worried

ANNOYED
aggravated
dismayed
disgruntled
frustrated
impatient
irritated
irked

ANGRY
furious
indignant
irate
livid
outraged
resentful

AVERSION
animosity
appalled
contempt
disgusted
dislike
horrified
hostile
repulsed

CONFUSED
ambivalent
baffled
bewildered
dazed
hesitant
mystified
perplexed
puzzled
torn

DISCONNECTED
alienated
aloof
bored
detached
distant
distracted
indifferent
numb
uninterested
withdrawn

DISQUIET
agitated
alarmed
disconcerted
perturbed
restless
startled
surprised
troubled
turbulent
turmoil
uncomfortable
uneasy
unsettled
upset

EMBARRASSED
ashamed
chagrined
flustered
guilty
mortified
self-conscious

FATIGUE
beat
burnt out
depleted
exhausted
lethargic
listless
sleepy
tired
weary
worn out

PAIN
agony
anguished
bereaved
devastated
grief
heartbroken
hurt
lonely
miserable
remorseful

SAD
depressed
despair
despondent
disappointed
discouraged
forlorn
hopeless
melancholy
unhappy
wretched

TENSE
anxious
cranky
distressed
distraught
irritable
nervous
overwhelmed
restless
stressed out

VULNERABLE
fragile
guarded
insecure
reserved
sensitive

YEARNING
envious
jealous
longing
nostalgic
wistful

RULES AND GUIDELINES FOR A SUCCESSFUL & TRANSFORMATIVE LIFE

- Growing and enriching *relationships,* and the *people* in relationship is the purpose.

- Loving means that others' needs, feelings, opinions and happiness are as important as my own.

- Nobody wins unless everybody wins, and never at the expense of another.

- No blame or judgment of another: giving one another the benefit of the doubt.

- Treat one another with the same love and respect you want to receive.

- Listen with curiosity and *intention* to appreciate and understand.

- Seek first to understand and second to be understood.

- Honesty involves telling your truth in **this** moment, not grievances of the past.

- Ego is selfish and has a closed heart.

- Defensiveness, criticism, resistance and contempt are the enemies of relationship.

- When you are sure you are right or need to be—you are usually wrong (EGO is driving).

- Problems offer possibilities, the real problem is limiting beliefs, feelings, attitudes.

- Miracles occur with shift in perspective and appreciating another's viewpoint.

RULES AND GUIDELINES FOR A SUCCESSFUL & TRANSFORMATIONAL EXPERIENCE

The guidelines for effective communication prohibit raising past hurts, offenses, and regrets during an unrelated discussion. There may be unresolved issues that still have juice in them, but save them until you have competed this program. When you have finished Dynamic Marriage, take a look at what needs to be cleared and discuss them with the skills and in the spirit of what you have learned.

The goal is to take a fresh—and gentle look at what unconscious factors you are currently operating under. Consider whether they still serve you well, then rewrite, refine, and agree on how you will handle things moving forward.

- Growing and enriching our marriage.

- Growing each *individual* in our relationship.

- Your needs, feelings, opinions, happiness are as important as mine.

- Nobody wins unless everybody wins, and never at your expense.

- No blame or judgment: always giving you the benefit of the doubt.

- I treat you with the same love and respect I want to receive.

- I listen with curiosity and *intention* to appreciate and understand.

- I seek *first* to understand and second to be understood.

- My ego is the enemy of openness and honesty.

- Control destroys love and intimacy.

- When I am sure I am right or need to be—I am probably wrong.

- Every problem/issue offers an array of possibilities & opportunities

- The biggest problem is limiting beliefs, expectations & attitudes.

- Miracles can be a slight shift in perspective to another's viewpoint

LOVED AND SPECIAL LIST EXERCISE

Loved & Special List (L & S)

This exercise seems so simplistic it is easy to discount it. On the contrary, it is the basis for all that follows in making your marriage everything you dream. Don't underestimate and neglect it. Use it consistently to have a profound effect on making your partner the center of your life. Cultivate this simple habit, it can set you on the road to the loving connection you want. This connection is the first compass point.

Make a L & S list:

- Each of you make a list of at least thirty things that make you feel Loved & Special.

- List things your partner has done and add things you wish he or she would do.

- The L & S list is meant to be a living, "dynamic" document most effective when consistently used, expanded, and updated.

> Download a monthly grid for this exercise at
> www.DiscoveringDynamicMarriage.com

- Make a date in the next week to share and exchange your lists with each other.

Ideas of things to put on your L & S list:

- Favorite romantic dates, affectionate words that touched you, expressions of love, appreciation, validation, and support.

- Add new things your partner does that you really like, such as: romantic gestures, affectionate words, a juicy kiss, celebration—the possibilities are endless—make a big deal of it.

Categories

Assign a category to each item on your L&S list from below. Total each category and place the number in the bottom line. This will give you an idea of how your beloved receives love. Lovers have been seeking a way into the beloved's heart from the beginning of time...here it is!

P = Physical contact: affection, PDA, sex

A = Attention: validation, appreciation, listening, emotional support,

V = Verbal: communication, compliments, discussing things

G = Gifts: presents, surprises, date nights, special effort

T = Thoughtfulness: consideration, sensitive gestures, personal services, honoring special occasions, awareness of matters important to spouse, interest in spouse's activities.

S = Shared experiences: vacations, recreation, activities, classes, couple's therapy, marriage enrichment

How to use your L & S list:

Every day, choose one item from your partner's list to give as a gift. You can't go wrong if it's on the list. Have fun with it.

Look for chances to surprise. Take risks. Be grateful. Cultivate your appetite for delight and wonder. Nurture curiosity. This is no place for egos!

If you remember nothing else...remember this: SURPRISE & CURIOSITY. These two elements that make children so charming and delightful will keep your relationship eternally spontaneous, exciting and juicy!

LOVED & SPECIAL CHECKLIST

Check the statements that are true for you.

☐ I consistently give a gift from my partner's L & S list every day.

☐ I always appreciate and acknowledge my partner's gifts from my L & S list.

☐ I usually answer my phone when my partner calls.

☐ I am eager to share significant events in my life with my partner at the end of the day.

☐ If I'm on a call when my partner calls, I usually return the call ASAP.

☐ My partner and I talk about personal things—not scheduling— at least once a day.

☐ I am physically and/or verbally affectionate with my partner every day.

☐ At social functions I like spending at least half the time interacting with my partner.

☐ I interrupt whatever I am doing to connect with my partner when they return home.

☐ Upon returning home, the first thing I do is check in with my partner.

☐ I enjoy time interacting with my partner more than reading or watching TV.

☐ I enjoy time with my partner more than other person in my life.

☐ When my partner wants my attention, I make it my priority.

☐ I generally rely on my partner when I need to talk something over.

☐ I celebrate my partner's birthday, our anniversary, and other special days.

☐ My partner and I go on a date alone at least once per week.

☐ My partner and I go on a romantic trip alone at least once per year.

☐ I have photographs of my partner in my office, wallet and/or cell phone.

☐ I engage in a meaningful discussion with my partner at least once a week.

☐ I look for opportunities to surprise and delight my partner each week.

HOW HEALTHY IS MY RELATIONSHIP?

Check the statements that are true for you.

☐ My good feelings about myself depend on being loved by you.

☐ Feeling good about myself is dependent on your approval.

☐ Your struggle upsets my tranquility.

☐ I am absorbed with solving your problems or relieving your pain.

☐ I am obsessed with pleasing you.

☐ I am preoccupied with protecting you.

☐ My self-esteem is bolstered by solving your problems.

☐ My self-esteem is supported by relieving your pain.

☐ My own hobbies and interests are abandoned in favor of yours.

☐ Your personal appearance must meet my standards because you are a reflection of me.

☐ Your behavior must meet with my approval because you are a reflection of me.

☐ How I feel is less important to me than how you feel.

☐ I am concerned with what you want more than with what I want.

☐ I am not aware of what is real—I assume what I want to believe is true.

☐ My dreams for the future are linked to you.

☐ My giving to you is an exchange for you fulfilling my expectations.

☐ What I do and say is compelled by my fear of rejection.

☐ Fear of your disapproval controls me.

☐ My fear of your anger governs what I do and say.

☐ I give as a way of feeling needed and secure in our relationship.

☐ My own social circle and activities diminish as my involvement with you increases.

☐ I compromise my own values in order to connect with you and gain your approval.

☐ I consider your opinion and way of doing things more important than my own.

☐ My quality of life is in direct relation to the quality of yours.

☐ My satisfaction with life is in direct relation to your satisfaction with life.

☐ My happiness is in direct proportion to your happiness.

This is an awareness exercise. A differentiated or self-referenced person would not have checked any of them. No one is perfect. The purpose is to notice the items you have checked and become more aware of your fusion beliefs and behaviors.

EMOTIONAL TRAUMA & LOSS HISTORY

Name: _____ Date: _____

The body stores painful memories that the mind may repress if it is not developed enough to process it. Such memories can undermine relationships and optimal functioning. Traumatic emotional and physical events, losses and injuries in the present can trigger repressed memories and interfere with emotional growth.

	AGE	DETAILS
Adoption		
Abandonment		
Addiction: you/family		
Parent anxiety/ depression		
Family secrets		
Unwanted pregnancy		
Emotional abuse		
Physical abuse		
Sexual abuse		
Spiritual/religious abuse		
Parental divorce		
Frequent moves		
Multiple caretakers		
Unstable/chaotic home		
Domestic violence		
Serious illness: you/ family		
Hospitalization		
Accident		
Natural disaster		

	AGE	DETAILS
Catastrophic event		
Parental death or illness		
Sibling death or illness		
Death of other child		
Physical/Sexual assault		
Over-controlling parents		
Indifferent parents		
Witnessed violence/ trauma		
Mental illness		

Additional information, memories comments:

_____

_____

_____

_____

_____

_____

_____

_____

_____

_____

_____

_____

_____

FAMILY OF ORIGIN SCRIPT ANALYSIS (FOOSA)

Purpose of the FOOSA

The cover of *Discovering a Dynamic Marriage* promises *12 Secrets to Navigating Uncharted Seas* of relationship. Inside there are twelve chapters covering twelve basic areas of marriage. It defines a new paradigm for success in intimate relationships. The secrets, however, are hidden in you. You have embedded scripts that form the beliefs and experiences underlying your relationship behaviors in each of the twelve areas of marriage, and so does your spouse. The voyage toward a lush and lively relationship in is based on identifying and understanding how the embedded scripts dictate the behaviors that undermine what you want in your marriage.

Instructions for using the FOOSA

You and your partner should prepare these separately. Whatever chapter you are working on, recall the early messages and behaviors that formed your beliefs about the subject matter of each chapter. Think about what you learned from your mother, and from your father. This analysis should include gender roles, attitudes, beliefs and behavior you learned and observed in your family of origin.

You and your partner share your FOOSA's. Many couples roar with recognition when they see tangible evidence of the reasons they have had conflict in this specific area. All of us follow the unconscious scripts and models from our early years, we have no other choice as long as they remain silent and unseen.

Benefits of the FOOSA

Exposing the unconscious scripts gives you a choice; the freedom to write your own script and choose your own destiny for your relationship and family. The exercise also generates understanding and facilitates letting go of old hurts and resentments resulting from embedded beliefs. We don't know what we don't know! It is easier to forgive someone acting out of ignorance or faulty beliefs. Granting a clean slate allows you to move forward in your relationship from an open heart and a forgiving spirit.

Use the FOOSA in any area you wish, but make a practice of doing it in an area that has been a source of conflict in your relationship. It is also useful for getting unstuck and/or back on track. When you fall into old patterns and things begin to get heated…stop…review the Rules & Guidelines and do a FOOSA to get you back on track.

FAMILY OF ORIGIN SCRIPT ANALYSIS (FOOSA)

Mother	Father

Wife

FAMILY OF ORIGIN SCRIPT ANALYSIS (FOOSA)

Mother	Father

Husband

PART SIX

INFORMATION & RESOURCES

ABOUT THE AUTHOR

Joy Evans Peterson, M.A. has been an agent of individual, marital, family, and organizational transformation for three decades. She is committed to lush and lively relationships and environments that transcend the commonplace and support enthusiasm and commitment in personal and family life. She helps couples co-author vibrant visions of the future to revitalize their marriage and create a nurturing environment for their children.

Joy has a life-long commitment to individuals, couples and families. Ms. Peterson has written Discovering a Dynamic Marriage, a life-changing program for couples struggling to keep their marriage vital in a society in which more than half of marriages fail. As a psychotherapist in private practice for over two decades, she has seen the long-term damage on children of divorce, according to research revealing that the negative effects are not transitory, but lifelong.

The author has four grown children, an adopted daughter and four grandchildren. She was raised in Southern California but has lived in the Pacific Northwest since 1977.

Ms. Peterson holds a Master's Degree in Clinical Psychology from Pepperdine University. She has undertaken post-graduate study in human and organizational systems and leadership development. She has been a presenter and participant in summits and conferences supporting a leadership role for women and youth.

The personal mission statement that has guided Joy's life for many years:

"Living so other whose lives brush mine

cherish life more for that moment in time."

ABOUT APPRECIATIVE INQUIRY

Discovering a Dynamic Marriage has its process roots in the principles of an organizational development model, Appreciative Inquiry (AI). The author discovered AI during post-graduate studies in Organizational Renewal many years ago. It is the most effective and respectful system in the field. Applying the model in a mental health practice, which she has been doing for over 20 years, has been transformative.

AI believes that "words create worlds." What you think about, you will talk about, and the words you use eventually manifest in your reality. It is consistent with the Scripture injunction that "as a man thinketh so is he." This truth is particularly relevant in intimate relationships, and is emphasized again and again in *Discovering a Dynamic Marriage*.

Another AI concept is that a better future should be built on a foundation of the best moments and practices of the past rather than the problems and failures. Most change systems focus on dealing with what isn't working. AI teaches that concentrating on what is working well and expanding it gradually crowds out what doesn't work.

Discovering a Dynamic Marriage applies these concepts to the most significant relationships in our lives—marriage and family. Mastering the positive approach will necessarily carry over to all relationships in life. The skills are basically what we consider leadership skills.

In a nutshell, the principles of Appreciative Inquiry can be summed up in four short questions. Some version of these questions can replace criticism, negativity and conflict in most situations.

1. What do you like about what is? What is working well? Tell me about a time when you were successful, excited, happy....

2. What would you like to have more of? What would you like to do differently? What can you glean from past successes to apply to the current challenge?

3. How can I support you? What do you need from me? How can I help?

4. What is your first step toward the outcome you desire?

Try it on everything...it works!

ABOUT THE BOOK

This book is the summation of Joy Peterson's four decades of counseling, coaching, and consulting. Whatever the setting, the emphasis is always on the quality of relationships. "It's all about relationships…only relationships" is her standard line.

When the recession hit in 2008, the demand for couple's counseling overwhelmed her church counseling center's capacity to respond. Couples are tricky even for a trained professional and only three mature couples were members who could be entrusted with the job. It wasn't unusual for a troubled couple to sit for four to six months on a waiting list to be assigned to a counselor.

This situation was resolved with the sessions that would become *Discovering A Dynamic Marriage*—unnamed at that point. The sessions and book initially evolved out of Joy's history with therapy groups. In the 1970s, the height of the "human potential" movement, groups were all the rage. Joy was involved in leading five groups a week for seven years with several male co-therapists. She was convinced from firsthand experience of the power of the synergy and healing that occurs in groups. She began wondering whether it was possible to treat couples in groups without exposing them. In the late 1990s, she retired from private practice to return to pursue post-graduate studies in organizational transformation and renewal.

While in graduate school, Joy came across an Organizational Development model that captured her attention. Appreciative Inquiry (AI) encapsulated everything she believed about healthy relationships being the heartbeat of every human endeavor. For ten years, Joy consulted with all types of organizations using Appreciative Inquiry as the exceptionally successful model.

Armed with AI, Joy returned to her early therapeutic roots in group settings and began to explore a model for treating couples in groups as large as twelve. She invited Dana and John Clauson, a retired Lutheran minister and two other couples to participate in a six-month pilot run of the program to try it out. Two of the couples had been married upwards of forty years and the other was reconciling after an eighteen-month separation in their twenty year marriage.

The Clausons and the other senior couple were retired ministers with considerable experience in mental health settings. Dana is a triage nurse who had trained as a lay counselor. Both couples felt secure in their marriages and were willing to be guinea pigs, not because they felt any personal anxiety about their relationships, but because they were aware of the need at the church and were caring folks. The pilot group exceeded everyone's expectations, especially Joy's.

The following September, Joy started a group with twelve couples, with the Clausons as facilitators-in-training. After four sessions, the Clausons had proven to be so competent that Joy withdrew to concentrate on writing the book and turned the group over to the Clausons. They continued to meet every week for several hours to prepare for the evening class. Those coaching sessions became the framework for the book…they *are* the book!

After the course ended, the Clausons continued to meet with Joy each Monday afternoon for at least three hours to go over the chapter she had written that week. They were her accountability partners. Their passion for and belief in the program inspired her when she felt too discouraged or too exhausted to write another word.

Somewhere between the pilot group and the first official group, Dana came up with the idea for the name. *Dare to Discover a Dynamic Marriage* was the working title, but it proved too cumbersome for the cover. The title was shortened to the present version, but you may notice Joy was unable to abandon the element of risk that *Dare* adds to the formula. Dare conveys the risk and courage involved in a voyage across uncharted seas throughout these pages.

On another note, if you wondered about the basis for the seafaring metaphor for marriage, it came out of a personal experience of courage in the face of life-threatening conditions. At the age of sixty-five, Joy was invited by a professor friend of hers to join her in an adventure she had dreamed about. Along with two men in their sixties who were experienced sailors, the woman skipper (the professor) age fifty-three, and Joy who was inexperienced other than a nineteen-foot ski boat. They set out from Seattle on the summer equinox crewing a forty-two-foot Morgan ketch on a sixteen-day blue water voyage to Ensenada, Mexico.

One hundred miles out in the Pacific Ocean off the coast of Oregon, they encountered a storm packing 65 knot wind and twenty-five foot waves, which continued unabated for thirty-six hours! "Spending a day and a half with your life literally hanging in the balance changes your perspective on how little control you have over what really matters," Joy reports. Summarizing the thirty-six hours, Joy laughingly describes, "Think four adults in a clothes dryer!"

When Joy began this book, the experience that kept coming back was the voyage. It illustrated the rough seas, flat calms, and rogue waves that occur in any lasting relationship...but also the magic—of dolphins dancing in your bow wake, the delight of flying fish in formation alongside, and the astonishing sight of a brilliantly lit city approaching out of the blackness of the midnight watch as a gigantic cruise ship slides by. Then only the sea, the stars, the moon, the sails filled with the invisible wind...*and the security of radar and GPS*. Now you know the inside story!

DISCOVERING A DYNAMIC MARRIAGE IN YOUR CHURCH OR ORGANIZATION

The Six-Month Course

Dynamic Marriage is at its most amazing as a course for 8-12 couples. Generally the course consists of 12 sessions meeting every other week over six months. Couples can really change their relationship over six months working together and with the group. The couples become bonded and supportive of one another on the months-long journey together.

The organizations that sponsor *Discovering a Dynamic Marriage* courses are churches and groups focused on families and children, such as YMCA and Boys & Girls Clubs. We generally open with a well-publicized one day workshop for 75-100 couples described below. Several churches or organizations can form a coalition to sponsor this as a service to the community.

The Workshop

The *Discovering a Dynamic Marriage* workshop is a one day event, an open invitation to couples in the community. We encourage sponsors to distribute invitation flyers to day care centers, pre-schools, aftercare centers and churches. Local newspapers are generally eager to publish an interview or article promoting the event as a community service. Parents with school-aged children are the prime candidates for this program.

Couples who attend the workshop will come away with important support for their marriage. They will have several options to move forward: they can go home with the book and the workbook to work on their own or with a family therapist, or they can sign up for the course at one of the sponsoring organizations. We provide promotional materials and media interviews.

The Website

The website is a continually evolving resource for couples and families. It offers a calendar of events, articles, links to other resources, special reports and relevant updates. There is an interactive blog for the online community to connect with one another, share their stories, celebrate their victories, ask questions of the author. The blog provides a way for couples to stay connected and get help when they encounter snags. The author monitors the blog conversations and weighs in on threads of interest to the community.

SPEAKING, PRESENTING, CONSULTING & COACHING

Joy Peterson is an engaging and dynamic Speaker or Presenter for events and conferences. She is also an experienced consultant and effective coach. She is available for speaking engagements, keynotes or breakout sessions at conferences for church leaders and mental health professionals, workshops, seminars and retreats. She addresses issues relevant to the themes of most conferences and events within the Appreciative Inquiry paradigm. As an example, she has written, presented or consulted on the following topics:

Relationships

- Intimate

- Parenting

- Sibling Rivalry

- Workplace

Healthy Workplace Environments

- Leadership

- Human Resources Effectiveness

- Constructive Performance Evaluations

- Team-building

- Targeted Hiring

Whole System Change Initiatives

- System Transparency

- Flattened Hierarchy

- Large Group Summit Process

Churches and Religious Organizations

- Discovering a Dynamic Marriage

- The Congregational Congress (whole system change)

- Developing a Lay Counseling Center

- Interfaith Relations

- Church Coalitions for Community Outreach

Contact Joy through either of these websites:

www.JoyEvansPeterson.com
or
www.DiscoveringDynamicMarriage.com

END NOTES

INTRODUCTION

1. Schnarch, David. *Passionate Marriage*. W. W. Norton & Company; Reprint edition (April 27, 2009). p.47

2. Transcendence: going beyond ordinary limits; surpassing; exceeding

3. Williamson, Marianne, *A Return to Love*, Harper Collins Publishers, Inc., 1992 p. xx.

4. Byron Katie, The Work www.thework.com/index. php

5. Mark 12:31

6. Philippians 4:11

PART I

Secret #1

1. Wallerstein: article summarizes her life and twenty-five years of research into the aftermath of divorce on children www.nytimes.com/2012/06/21/health/research/judith-s-wallerstein-psychologist-who-analyzed-divorce-dies-at-90.html

2. Wallerstein, Judith S. et al. . New York: Hyperion, 2000. p. xxvii

3. Ibid

4. Welwood, John. *Intimate Relationship as a Spiritual Crucible.* p. 1 www.johnwelwood.com/articlesandinterviews.htm

5. Gottman, John et al. Cambridge, MA: Bradford Books, 2002.

6. *Waking up in Relationship*, Interview with John Welwood by Pam Burton of KPFK www.johnwelwood.com/articlesandinterviews.htm

Secret #2

1. Lindbergh, Anne Morrow. *Gift from the Sea.* New York, New York: Pantheon Books/Random House, 1975. p 104.

2. Matthew 7:12 and Mark 12:31

3. Schnarch, David. p. 51-52. www.passionatemarriage.com

4. Dissemble: a) to give a false or misleading appearance to; conceal the truth or real nature of: b) to put on the appearance of; feign:

5. Allender, Dan and Tremper Longman. *Bold Love.* Colorado Springs: Nav Press, 1992. p. 58

6. See I Corinthians 13, the classic Scripture passage for a definition of love, which includes humility and trust.

7. *The Emperor's New Clothes* by Hans Christen Anderson.

8. *Leadership and Self-Deception*, Arbinger Institute, Berrett-Koehler Publishers, Inc., San Francisco, CA, 2002. Preface

9. Quote attributed to an unpublished Mayan sage

10. Schnarch, David: an interview

11. Karen, Robert.

Secret #3

1. Backstory: the emotional history, experience, fears and underlying beliefs that give rise to Power and Control issues in your relationship.

2. Gottman's Four Horsemen, www.youtube.com/ watch?v=CbJPaQY_1dc

3. *How Healthy Is My Relationship* is an exercise shown in Part V. Tools & Illustrations, and is available as a Worksheet in the Dynamic Marriage Companion Workbook or as a download from the website: www. DiscoveringDynamicMarriage.com

Secret #4

1. Loved & Special assignment. Found in Part IV. Tools and Illustrations and as a download on www.DiscoveringDynamicMarriage.com

2. 1 John 4:18

3. Genesis 1:26-27

4. A phrase borrowed from the recovery field, Alcoholics Anonymous and Celebrate Recovery.

5. Circle of Security, www.circleofsecurity.net

6. Matthew 7:1

7. Gottman, John. www.gottman.com

8. Williamson, Marrianne. Lecture "On Intimacy"

PART II

Secret #5

1. en.wikipedia.org/wiki/Sugar_addiction

Secret #6

1. www.WhatMakesYouTick.com

2. See Emotional Trauma and Loss History in Part V

3. Sprecher, Susan, Ph.D., Psychologist, llinois State University. Article, "What's Love Got To Do With It," *Psychology Today*.www.psychologytoday.com/articles/199907/whats-love-got-do-it

Secret #7

1. Liturgy is the structure of a worship service. In Greek *Liturgy* means "the work of the people."

2. FOOSA= Family of Origin Script Analysis. Found in
    Part IV. Tools and Illustrations and as a download on
    www.DiscoveringDynamicMarriage.com

PART III

Secret #8

1. http://en.wikipedia.org/wiki/Father_Knows_Best
   Accessed August 4, 2012.

2. Hall, Ken. *Billy Gray, Bud from Father Knows Best
   Collects Racing Motorcylcles.* Gostar.com 4/30/10

3. Gloria Steinem was an early feminist is credited
   along with Betty Freidan of forming the National
   Women's Political Caucus, which worked on behalf
   of women's issues. She was also one of the founders
   of . Magazine. www.biography.com/people/glo-
   ria-steinem-9493491

Secret #9

1. Ted Ownby, *American Dreams in Mississippi: Con-
   sumers, Poverty, and Culture 1830-1998* (University
   of North Carolina Press, 1999)

Secret #10

1. Gladwell, Malcolm.

2. From a review on Amazon.com. "Malcolm Gladwell
   takes us on an intellectual journey through the world
   of "outliers"--the best and the brightest, the most
   famous and the most successful. He asks the ques-

famous and the most successful. He asks the question: what makes high-achievers different?

His answer is that we pay too much attention to what successful people are like, and too little attention to where they are from: that is, their culture, their family, their generation, and the idiosyncratic experiences of their upbringing.

Examining the lives of outliers from Mozart to Bill Gates, he builds a convincing case for how successful people rise on a tide of advantages, "some deserved, some not, some earned, some just plain lucky."

PART IV

Secret #11

1. Siegel, Daniel and Mary Hartzell. *Parenting From The Inside Out.* New York: Penguin, 2004. p. 4

2. Ibid, p. 5

3. Belluck, Pam. "In Study, Fatherhood Leads to Drop in Testosterone." *New York Times.* September 11, 2011.

4. Gottman, John. *The Mathematics Of Love* Interview.